*School Business
Administration*

THE LIBRARY OF EDUCATION

A Project of The Center for Applied Research in Education, Inc.

G. R. Gottschalk, Director

Categories of Coverage

I	II	III
Curriculum and Teaching	Administration, Organization, and Finance	Psychology for Educators

IV	V	VI
History, Philosophy, and Social Foundations	Professional Skills	Educational Institutions

School Business

Administration

LEO M. CASEY

Assistant Superintendent for Business
Garden City Public Schools

The Center for Applied Research in Education, Inc.
New York

Foreword

Public education in this nation is big business in terms of goals and objectives, number of people involved, and financial investment.

This book, dealing with school business administration, starts with the premise that the basic job of the schools is to instruct, and that the many operational and auxiliary services which normally are considered part of "school business" are designed to help expedite instruction and to serve related professional objectives of the schools. The business department as a whole, or the minor individual segments of the business service, are not intended to be masters but, rather, servants of the educational enterprise.

Dr. Casey has demonstrated a high level of competence as a professionally prepared person and is actively engaged in the field of school administration, with special interest in the related areas of business. He presents in this volume an excellent overview of the philosophy supporting this specialized area of service, and also gives the reader extensive information concerning the better practices involved in carrying on school business affairs. Actually, this volume is more than a mere overview: the reader will be able to derive much more than a mere acquaintance with the individual areas of school business.

This volume can be read advantageously by administrators, who may gain new insights, but it also should appeal to a host of principals, teachers, and lay persons who want to get a good appreciation of the fundamentals of school business administration without having to wade through voluminous tomes. The fundamentals are here, and are very well described.

HENRY H. LINN

Professor of Education, Emeritus
Teachers College, Columbia University

v

School Business Administration

Leo M. Casey

This book is a concise presentation of the practice of school business administration. For those who desire an overview of this important service aspect of administration, the present volume is most
welcome. Such topics as the role of the business administrator, the
budget, accounting, purchasing, insurance, operation and maintenance, transportation, and food service are defined, analyzed
briefly, and illustrated by the literature on these subjects as well as
by the broad background and experience of the author.

Dr. Leo Casey is the Assistant Superintendent for Business in the
Garden City, New York, School District. He received his graduate
education at Teachers College, Columbia University, has had wide
experience in school business management, and is prominent in state
and national associations of school business administrators.

DANIEL E. GRIFFITHS
Content Editor

Contents

CHAPTER IV

Purchasing 53

CHAPTER V

Insurance 67

CHAPTER VI

Operation and Maintenance 79

CHAPTER I

The Mission of School Business Management

School Business Management

Definition and objective. School business management may be defined as that phase of educational administration which has as its major responsibility the provision of funds and facilities essential for the attainment of the educational goals of the school system.

School business management deals with people (pupils, staff members, and public) as well as with things (buildings, equipment, and supplies). It is important to understand that the business management function cannot be isolated from the other activities of the school system. This function, properly conducted, is related to all the other aspects of the school enterprise.

School business management is a service function: it seeks to provide a setting and climate that will enhance instruction. In itself it has neither end nor justification; its need and direction must be evaluated by its contribution to the teaching-learning process.

Thus, the objective of school business management is to assist in the realization of the educational goals of the school system. The complex modern school system will progress more rapidly when the business aspects are administered soundly and competently.

Areas of responsibility. The areas of responsibility of business management vary with local conditions. State laws, local custom, the size and type of district, and the competency of administrative staff members are all determining factors. The major functions generally considered to be part of school business management are:

1. *Budget.* The budget is the reflection of the plans for the immediate school program. The thoroughness and accuracy of its development will have substantial effect on the achievements of the period covered. Expenditure requests for supplies, equipment, staff, facilities, and maintenance must be developed, analyzed, evaluated, and approved. After the budget has been approved and adopted, a

1

procedure must be evolved to implement it and a method of limiting substantial expenditures to those detailed in the document.

2. *Financial accounting.* This enterprise covers all the records of all funds in the custody of the school district and all its financial transactions. The general fund and the payroll fund are the major elements in value and volume. Usually, accounting methods are outlined in detail by state regulations. But the principles underlying the worthy stewardship of public funds are universal, and require prudence both in physical handling and in record keeping.

3. *Purchasing.* This area involves the 10–20 per cent of the school budget usually expended to procure materials and outside services. Since purchases range from textbooks to musical instruments to chemicals to school buses, it is essential that the acquisition process be soundly managed. Incompetent management means the waste of large sums of money. In addition, it may impinge on the educational program because it may lead to the purchase of materials which do not possess the qualities needed. This is a sensitive area of management for two other reasons. One is the fact that state laws mandate certain purchasing procedures, such as public bidding for contracts in which sizable amounts of money are involved. The other is the hazard of dishonest practices, which is always present when a large volume of money is involved.

4. *Supply management.* Supply management is the orderly management of supplies and equipment from the time they are purchased and delivered until they are to be utilized. The complexity of this function is usually related to the size of district: larger districts ordinarily have substantial stores operations. A major consideration in supply management is whether to maintain central warehousing or to decentralize the storage of materials in individual schools. Some districts combine both methods, centralizing certain items and decentralizing others. Regardless of the method of warehousing, care must be exercised in stockpiling and distributing supplies and equipment, which are school district assets of considerable monetary value.

5. *Insurance.* Since the value of even a medium-sized school district's properties may be between twenty and fifty million dollars, care must be taken to protect against catastrophic financial loss. This protection is usually afforded by securing fire insurance. In ad-

dition, there are many other forms of insurance—particularly liability coverage—which have a place in the portfolios of many schools. Because of the complexity of insurance policies, a number of districts have been underprotected or overprotected. Another consideration vital to the sound management of the insurance program is the method of placing insurance. More and more school districts are finding it advantageous to secure informal bids before contracting for insurance coverage.

6. *Plant operations.* This includes the daily housekeeping of structures and grounds and relates principally to the work of the custodial force. With the increased recognition of the need for a healthful environment, schools are more conscious of custodial service. Further, the modern school is more complicated and has greater amounts of space per pupil. Thus, present-day custodial operations are more complex, requiring more planning and more technical knowledge at both the working and supervisory levels.

7. *Maintenance of plant.* This function deals with periodic and long-term programs of protecting, preserving, and restoring the physical plant. Once a building is erected, it can be properly utilized only if it is well maintained. To skimp on maintenance is to limit the degree to which the structure will be usable, and may eventually lead to greater dollar expenditures. So-called deferred maintenance frequently leads to excessive costs because deterioration is progressive.

8. *Transportation.* As America took to the road, so did the school districts. For better or worse, public schools have generally been given the responsibility of transporting pupils to and from instruction. This adds up to the largest transportation enterprise in the nation. At the local level it means problems, planning, decisions, and sizable costs. A frequent question is: "Should the district own its own transportation fleet?" Typically the answer has been "Yes," and the percentage of district-owned fleets is growing. However, there are cases where contracting with a private carrier is more advantageous. The kind and quality of service must be decided by the school board, but the management of the transportation complex is an administrative task of considerable magnitude.

9. *Food service.* The provision of hot lunches in school goes back many years, but the movement has had its greatest growth since the end of World War II. Much impetus for the growth was fur-

nished by the federal government's substantial program of food and cash subsidies. Today the school cafeteria may be the largest restaurant in town. Most schools undertake the entire enterprise with their own facilities and staff. However, some schools favor contracting for the services of a caterer, who staffs and manages the school's kitchen.

10. *Personnel management.*   In most schools the business office must perform certain personnel management functions which apply to all staff members. For the professional staff, these functions typically involve notifying personnel of salary schedules, accounting for sick leave and retirement credit, and paying salaries each pay period. For noncertificated or supporting staff members such as office workers, custodians, and maintenance personnel, the list is broadened to include recruitment, selection, appointment, and in-service training. The increasing complexity of fringe benefits and the growing recognition of the need for programs of securing and retaining competent personnel are causing growth in the personnel management function.

11. *Construction.*   New public schools are being erected at a total annual cost in excess of three billion dollars. Except in the very largest school districts, architectural and engineering services for such construction are typically provided by private firms. However, there are many undertakings, such as the construction of small additions and the making of alterations, for which the business manager frequently has a direct responsibility. In either case, the business office should be able to provide assistance in planning, to insure that the completed structure will be educationally functional and operationally economical.

12. *Financial reporting.*   Reporting to the governing body is an obligation of good management. In local school districts, many of the financial reports are dictated by state law or regulation. Without the intelligence furnished by financial reports, the superintendent, the board of education, and the public cannot have the knowledge required to make sound decisions. The business office should have the raw material necessary for any financial report. In discharging this function, the goal is to design report formats that are meaningful.

13. *Debt service management.*   Few school districts are able to construct needed facilities on a pay-as-you-go basis; thus, they bor-

row capital and repay it over a period of years. The selection of the type of bond to be issued and the timing of the issue are major decisions requiring careful evaluation, since these decisions commit the district for twenty or thirty years. The periodic payment of principal and interest is generally a matter of routine, fixed at the time the bonds are issued. The credit rating of the district depends, to a degree, on the prompt and regular payment of its debt.

14. *Cost analysis.* A school administration must ask itself what a particular facet of the program costs and what it is worth. With the mounting cost and complexity of public education, the question is asked more and more often. A part of the answer—the cost in dollars—can be furnished by a well-organized business office.

15. *Long-term planning.* This should include consideration of program, staff, facilities, and fiscal matters. In a way, long-term planning is merely budget planning over an extended period, usually five or ten years. It is an essential device for efficient realization of educational goals and long-term plans should be revised each year or two. Too many districts, caught in the pressure of developing annual budgets, fail to project their program beyond the next year. Of necessity, this function must involve the entire staff, but its coordination is frequently assigned to the business office.

Guidelines to organization and operation. In any colloquy on management, the observer rapidly reaches the point where he desires to establish basic principles. A study of school business management is no different, except that we are less sure of what may be called a "principle." We cannot yet be confident that many of our effective rules are indeed principles, for they may not yet have undergone the needed study, testing, and evaluation. Nevertheless, we do have some solid generalizations which can serve as guidelines and be presented with confidence, so long as their limitations are recognized. Among these are the following:

1. The business management function exists to improve the setting of the educational program.

2. The task to be done is defined in relation to objectives.

3. Individual tasks are integrated for the achievement of common goals.

4. As tasks are defined, ample manpower is provided to insure their realization.

5. Authority is clearly assigned in order to avoid duplication of effort and indecision.

6. Effective fiscal controls are maintained so that public funds are treated as a public trust.

7. Long-range planning, financial and functional, is an integral part of current operations.

8. Provision is made to evaluate procedures and to make such revision and elimination as may be needed.

9. To the degree possible, policy development involves all those affected by the action.

10. Relationships with vendors are maintained on the highest level of ethical business practice.

11. Decisions are made on the basis of educational efficiency as well as dollar economy.

12. Coordination of individual efforts is the responsibility of the business administrator.

13. No staff member is required to take direct orders from more than one superior.

14. Staff members are recognized for their individual worth and encouraged to grow through in-service programs, promotion, and participation in regional, state, and national groups.

15. Salary, fringe benefits, and job conditions are competitive with the economy and commensurate with the caliber of staff member required for the position.

16. Policies are so stated that they permit some flexibility in application.

17. Authority needed to achieve the desired results is granted simultaneously with the assignment of task.

18. Organizational structure emphasizes simplicity, with work effort centered in small task forces.

The School Business Administrator

Present status.   There are wide variances in the methods used by school districts to accomplish business management functions. In the smallest districts, the superintendent acts as business administrator, along with his other roles. The slightly larger district typically has an assistant superintendent for business or a business manager who performs, or supervises the performance of, these functions.

The largest school districts frequently have additional personnel who are assigned to areas of responsibility and report to the chief school business administrator. Frequently the staff includes a superintendent of buildings and grounds, a cafeteria director, a purchasing agent, and an accounting officer.

However, the difference between the business management function in a smaller district and the same function in a larger district is principally a matter of the amount rather than the kind of activity. For example, sound purchasing practice in a small district follows the same basic steps as in a large district, even though the quantity and variety of purchases is considerably smaller.

Perhaps the distinguishing feature of administrators in charge of school business management is the abundance of different titles by which they are known. The two most common designations are Assistant Superintendent for Business and Business Manager. Hill's survey [1] showed the following additional titles in use:

Administrative Assistant	Clerk-Treasurer
Clerk	Superintendent of Buildings
Director of Business Affairs	and Grounds
Controller	Secretary of Board of Education
Financial Secretary	Business Secretary

The duties of these incumbents understandably varies, but generally follow the list of functions outlined earlier. The experience and training of present chief school business administrators reflects a broad range of background. Some come to the position from related activity in industry; others advance from the ranks of teachers and school administrators. Although the baccalaureate degree is now considered minimal, education ranges from a high school diploma to post-doctoral training.

Emerging role. The extension of the school business administrator position to medium-sized and small school districts is largely a post-World War II phenomenon. This expansion was particularly evident in the 1950's when a great number of districts with between 2000 and 10,000 pupils created the position. The creation of a large number of new positions in a short span of years produced mixed results. In some cases, the local district carefully assayed the function and established job specifications for the position. Unfortunately, some districts recognized the need for a person to lead the

---

[1] Frederick W. Hill, "The Present Status of Certification of School Business Officials," *School Business Affairs,* Vol. 24, No. 3 (March, 1958), 3.

business function but did not define what talents were to be required of him.

This tremendous upsurge in demand has resulted in two broad-based studies of the emerging role of the school business administrator. In 1956, the Cooperative Development of Public School Administration in New York State published a report on *The School Business Administrator* [2] as part of a series on local school district administrative staffing. Although this report was addressed specifically to New York State school districts, its message has national application. In 1960 the Association of School Business Officials of the United States and Canada published a research report entitled *The School Business Administrator*.[3] This report had significance because it emanated from the international professional organization to which most school business officials belong.

The consensus of these reports, of other studies, and of qualified professionals is that the job is evolving and will change substantially in the years ahead. Perhaps the best way to synthesize current perceptions on the emerging profile of the school business administrator is to answer several pertinent questions.

1. *What should his training be?*   The school business administrator will be expected to have graduate-level education—at least the master's degree, but preferably including a sixth year of preparation. The graduate program should be undertaken only in those schools that have the staff, facilities, and students to develop quality programs for school business administration. The undergraduate program should be diversified and rigid specialization should be avoided. The graduate training should include a core of general education and administration course work, with emphasis on actual training in administration, rather than on a study of administration. This training should be enriched by a program in business management specifics, including accounting, law, school construction, operation and maintenance of plant, purchasing, budgeting, insurance, transportation, food service, and personnel management.

An internship program, in which the graduate student receives

---

[2] Cooperative Development of Public School Administration in New York State, *The School Business Administrator* (Albany, N.Y.: CDPSA, 1956).

[3] Association of School Business Officials of the United States and Canada, *The School Business Administrator* (Evanston, Ill.: The Association, 1960).

on-the-job experience in a controlled environment, should be included. Attention must also be given to the in-service education of school business administrators. The rapid advances in many areas of school business fully justify an active program of workshops, seminars, and conferences for the practitioner.

2. *What should his prior experience be?* Prior experience is usually important for the maturity that it should have nurtured. But all men do not mature at the same rate and all job experience is not of equal value. So it is hazardous to outline a parameter of prior experience.

To be most valuable, this experience should have been in public education (as a teacher or administrative assistant), in private enterprise, or in activity related to school business functions. The experience is enhanced by the degree to which it has involved administrative responsibility.

3. *What should his temperament be?* The job to be done is not impossible, so the man to do it does not have to be a superman. He needs the standard attributes of any administrator. These would include integrity, ability to work with others, interest in people, and emotional stability. As in other administrative jobs, vigor, a sense of priorities and objectives, a willingness to make decisions, and skill in communication are necessary.

Beyond this, the school business administrator must also have an interest in the business management aspects of education. This means a tolerance of the requirement for precision in much of his actions, because he is dealing with absolutes. It means a talent for living with deadlines and routines, because much of the activity consists of these.

4. *How large should a school district be before it seeks to create the position?* Chances are that the school district with 2000 or more pupils needs a school business administrator. If such a district does not have a business administrator, it is probably shortchanging its total operations in one of two ways. First, it could simply be failing to provide the leadership essential to the economical and efficient conduct of its business affairs. Second, it could be "stealing" the time of another administrator or administrators for the performance of these business functions, thus shortchanging some aspect of instructional leadership.

Necessarily, the 2000 figure is flexible. Many school districts with smaller enrollments have had business administrators for many years. A district whose enrollment is still below this minimum but growing rapidly may have urgent need to create the position. Districts of such growth typically have problems of building construction, equipment selection and purchasing, and staff expansion which require the assistance of a school business administrator.

5. *What is adequate compensation for the position?* This question presupposes that there is a cluster of compensations—monetary and nonmonetary—in any position. School business administration shares with other school administrative positions the attributes of stability, high status, and substantial challenges which can lead to achievement and satisfaction.

Currently the annual salary rates for these positions range from about $5000 to $30,000. Because of the wide variances in skill and responsibility among individuals, it would be difficult to sustain any claim that the range of salaries is unjust. Two factors enhance future prospects for continued improvement of this salary range. One is the almost universal recognition of the need for a significant improvement of teachers' salaries. Because teachers' wages are the base on which administrative salaries are decided, improvement of the one will probably lead to proportionate improvement of the other. Further, boards of education and school superintendents are aware that a competent business administrator can both serve educational aims and save money. To gain this double dividend, they are and will be increasingly willing to invest in a higher salary for the talented school business administrator.

6. *What should the required credentials be?* If the business administrator is designated assistant superintendent for business, he is usually required to qualify for the same educationally oriented certification as the superintendent of schools. New York and California are among those states which have a second, noneducational certificate for school business administrators, which usually brings with it the title of business manager. But there are a large number of positions that are occupied by individuals without any certification, owing either to an absence of state requirements or to an avoidance of them.

A model certificate would be one issued by the state agency

licensing teachers and should require at least a master's degree, but preferably a sixth year of preparation, with appropriate course emphasis. Full certification should require about five years of experience in teaching and administration. Although all evidence indicates the trend toward the appointment of assistant superintendents for business, justice demands the retention of credentials for the business manager. This could be achieved by providing a parallel certificate requiring equivalent training and experience for those who cannot meet the requirement of professional education.

CHAPTER II

The School Budget

Definition

The school budget is the blueprint of what the educational program will be and what it will cost. It predicts the expenditures necessary to support the program and identifies the amount and source of receipts needed to meet these expenditures. A sound budget is far more than a document; it is a vehicle. Thus its worth to the school is measured by the quality of the procedures used to design and implement a program rather than by the physical form of the printed document. The budget constitutes the vectors of action to be pursued by the school district during the period covered.

Many persons think of a budget as a plan developed annually for the year to come. It is true that most school districts address major concern to their annual budget. However, many of these districts will also be involved in all three types of school budgets.

1. *The annual budget* includes the current operating expenses, together with annual capital outlay and any debt service payments to be made during the period. Normally it covers a fiscal year, which in turn encompasses a full school year.

2. *The capital expenditure budget* includes expenditures for site purchases, building construction, and large-scale renovation projects. These activities—and therefore the budget—usually extend over several years and are most often financed by a bond issue.

3. *Long-range financial planning* is in the nature of a forecast of the combined annual and capital needs of the school district, projected over an extended period of time.

Purpose and Function

Continuous process. The school budget is the starting point of all educational, fiscal, and business activity in a school district. But the starting point is not noticed in a well-managed organization because budget making is a continuous process.

Quite properly, the serious planning of the succeeding year's annual budget is underway before more than a small fraction of the current year's budget has been expended. Concurrently, the alert district is evolving a revised long-term plan which encompasses the next several years and considering its capital expenditure needs. Experience with past annual budgets forms the basis for appraisals and estimates of present and future needs.

Legal requirements. Most states include in their laws a requirement that the local school district prepare an annual budget. In the majority of cases the state requirement includes prescriptions both for budget format and for the coding of revenues and expenditures. These requirements establish, at least generally, the method and content of the business office's accounting function.

The legal requirements for budgets for capital expenditures are usually less specific. Yet the magnitude of these expenditures and the significant interval between conception and completion justify care in planning. There is usually no general legal obligation to prepare long-range financial plans. However, districts involved in reorganization or in large building programs may be obliged to prepare long-range plans to satisfy state regulations.

The budget is generally initiated by the superintendent and his staff, adopted by the board of education, and approved by the public. In the case of capital expenditure budgets, voter approval may be necessary for any proposal concerning the issuance of bonds. In a few districts, annual budgets are approved through direct voting by residents. Voter approval of each component of the budget may be required in some districts; in others, voter approval may be required only in those cases where a proposed school tax rate exceeds a certain level.

Some school districts must present their annual budget proposals to local governmental agencies. For example, many city school districts are required to submit their budgets to a municipal board or commission for approval. This may involve only the granting of funds, or it may include approval of the program as well as of its financing. Certain noncity school districts may face the same requirement, submitting their budgets to town, township, or county government units for approval.

In a few cases the local school district may be required to submit its proposed budget to a department of the state government for approval of program and cost. When the approval of voters or a local noneducational agency is not a part of the endorsement process, it is not unusual to impose a tax limitation on the school district. Most of these ratifications are designed to guarantee the system of checks and balances in governmental operation, rather than to guarantee a particular level of educational program.

Tool of understanding. The budget can be a splendid device for expanding the understandings of staff, board of education, and patrons. Valuable insights can be afforded to staff members by their participation in the identification of needs, the translation of these needs into costs, the appraisal of potential income, the evaluation of the relative merits of different needs, and the establishment of budget priorities.

It soon becomes apparent to those who participate in drawing up a budget that the problem involves more than merely identifying worthy objectives. Any effective social enterprise must establish the direction and tempo of its movement and must arrange for regular evaluation of this movement. Beyond this, however, it must establish priorities. These priorities are critically important to school budgets because the school has only limited resources of staff and funds. The evaluation of different items and the assignment of priorities to each are crucial in building the budget. As Ovsiew and Castetter [1] state: "Although more money is always useful, what really counts is where the money is applied and the wisdom of its use."

Finally, the budget offers much to all citizens of the community: it identifies what the school system's goals shall be; it pinpoints shifts in emphasis; it expresses new needs and indicates how these will be met. It is the locus of plans, of program, of finance.

Guide for action. After they have been adopted and approved, both the annual budget and the capital expenditure budget become guides for action. The annual budget forms the basis for establishing the accounting records for the ensuing fiscal period, indicating both

---

[1] Leon Ovsiew and William B. Castetter, *Budgeting for Better Schools* (Englewood Cliffs, N.J.: Prentice-Hall, Inc., 1960), p. 34.

the nature and the extent of future expenditures. This budget also discloses the pattern of receipts to be obtained and the amount to be derived from the local tax levy.

Budgeting appropriations are the starting point for all expenditures. They identify the amount and kind of purchasing that may be undertaken. These allowances identify the kind and numbers of staff to be employed. In the case of an expanding staff, these allowances become the authorization to recruit additional personnel. The budget also indicates the salary rates to be paid all staff members.

Similarly, the final budget identifies the kind and amount of supplies and equipment to be secured. Thus, it sets the tempo for all purchasing activity. Maintenance, repair, and replacement projects, as well as capital construction and acquisitions, are undertaken on the basis of budgetary authorizations.

It is usual for state law to restrict school district expenditures to the budgetary total, unless an emergency arises. However, it is common for the statute to grant local boards of education the authority to transfer fund allowances from one to another of the various components of the total budget. This discretion is necessary lest the budget become the master, rather than the servant, of the program. Care must be taken to limit appropriation transfers to those that are essential and those that could not have been foreseen at the time the budget was prepared. Abuse of this privilege by the board of education may lead to public distrust of the management of the schools.

In this dimension, then, the adopted budget becomes a charter to those who manage the school district. It delineates the nature and extent of the expenditures to be made in a given fiscal period. This is not to say that a school district spends because the budget appropriated a specific sum for a specific object. Rather, the budget identifies the wide range of specific transactions that represent the school district's plan of action.

Annual Budget Procedures

Preparation.   The preparation of the annual budget involves the selective establishment of hundreds of accounts and subaccounts to cover both receipts and expenditures. The fact that the school district has few sources of income and that these usually have restrictions limits consideration of the receipts portion of the budget. Thus, the major effort is expended on determinations of expenditures. These judgments may be catalogued as involving either *staffing* or *overhead* decisions.

Staffing decisions. Staffing decisions underlie a large percentage of the costs in any annual budget. The school district determines between 80 and 90 per cent of its operating budget for a given period when it answers two questions.

1. *What will the level of staffing be?* This question seeks to determine needs for classroom teachers, special teachers, administrators, clerical personnel, custodians, bus drivers, and maintenance workers and the manner in which these personnel will be deployed. Can the district reduce class size? What are the effects of such a reduction on the budget and on the educational program? Should advanced instruction in science, mathematics, and languages be offered to extremely small groups of pupils? These small class sections are expensive, but are they not necessary to a diversified program?

Will the school district add more guidance counselors? More psychologists? Can it meet fully its obligations to the community unless it recognizes the need to expand this aspect of the program? Should it add two more groundsmen to maintain the front lawn or the athletic field? This question, then, may really be phrased as: "How many?"

2. *What will the compensation for staff be?* This question considers the salary and related benefits to be paid to staff members. Most of the conditions of service for those on the staff must be considered. Are the salary schedules enabling the school district to secure adequate numbers of personnel with desired skills, training, experience, and personality? Are the salary schedules providing just rewards for faithful and competent service?

Should an effort be made to reduce the number or to increase the amount of increments in salary? What should the district be doing about fringe benefits, the cost of which frequently accounts for as much as 20–25 per cent of the salary budget? What will be the impact—both on cost and on staff morale—of an increase in paid sick leave? What is the district's responsibility in sharing the costs of employees' health insurance and life insurance programs? This question, again involving all elements of the program, may be phrased as: "How much?"

These two questions are brief, but they must be considered at length for the responses have tremendous impact on the future operations of the school. Few of the school's goals can be realized without adding staff or altering staff responsibilities. An added complication is the simple fact that the cost of personnel is high and is increasing each year. If there is a standard failure in budget preparation, it is the inadequate consideration of problems of staffing and of their effect on program and finances.

Overhead decisions. Items of overhead expenditure constitute the second category of budgeting. Overhead consists largely of things, such as supplies, equipment, and outside services. Usually the overhead category will total about one fifth of the total annual budget. The overhead items in a budget can be assorted into absolute mandates, limited mandates, or free options.

Absolute mandates embrace those annual budget items that are included because of existing laws, regulations, or prior contract. These expenditures are necessary if the school district is to exist. The largest of the mandates is usually debt service: payments of interest and reduction of principal on earlier bond issues. Premiums for fire insurance or other kinds of insurance would be a mandated expense if the law required such coverage. The employer's share of Social Security and retirement system costs are other examples of mandated expenses. Where transportation service is required by state law, a contract to provide it is mandated.

Limited mandates include those expenditures which are not required by law or regulation but are dictated by sound business practices. This classification includes expenses for fuel, power, telephone service, pest control, water, auditing service, insurance other than that required by law, and surety bonds. Although these are not legal obligations, their use is demanded by practicality. The superintendent and his staff and the board of education may exercise their judgment in degree rather than in kind. This means they may decide not to insure every object for all potential hazards, but they may not fail to provide adequate protection for major hazards.

Options include those few budget items which the administration and the board can include or exclude or for which they can alter substantially the amount of the appropriation. Examples of options include textbooks and instructional supplies for students, library books, furniture replacement, painting, new and replacement instructional equipment, certain alterations, and nonmandated transportation. The decision could be made to eliminate any one of these items from the annual budget and the school district would still continue to function.

The effect that such an elimination or alteration would have on the program varies. In some cases elimination from the budget would merely transfer the obligation to the parents. An example of this would be textbooks and certain instructional supplies, which are sometimes purchased by the individual parents. On the other hand, failure to provide up-to-date library books and modern instructional equipment could only lead to damage to the instructional program. Furthermore, this action would require inordinate expenditures in some future annual budgets to make up for these deferred expenses.

An analysis of the overhead category reveals that the opportunities for significant judgments are indeed few. The entire category comprises only about 20 per cent of the total budget, most of which will be mandated by law or by good sense. Discretionary actions—that is, those dealing with options—are confined to considerably less than 10 per cent of the total budget, and here the judgments must be astute. If they are not, the school district may be injuring its long-term welfare.

The most important activity of the board of education in overhead expenditures is the development of perspective. It would be folly to presume that a large proportion of these costs are nonessential to education and can be eliminated or significantly reduced. Actually, the board has restricted liberty of judgment, for expenses must further program objectives previously accepted by the board.

Business office responsibility. The budget can be described by two terms: *program* and *means.* The program is what the school seeks to do in a given period of time. Program development is the primary professional responsibility of the superintendent and his subordinates and should be a major concern of the board of education. Means evolve from program and include the staff, services, supplies, equipment, and facilities required to carry out the program and the revenues to finance it.

The responsibility of the business administrator will be principally directed toward evolving the means aspect of the budget. Among the responsibilities typically assigned to the business administrator are the following:

1. Preparation and distribution of budget forms for use by all schools and departments. Care in developing the content of these forms will simplify subsequent purchasing procedures.

2. Coordination of the budgets submitted by individual schools or administrative units to avoid duplication and omission.

3. Development of cost estimates for proposals that would change the number of professional staff members or their compensation.

4. Development of proposals for changes in number of or compensation for nonprofessional or supporting staff members.

5. Submission of data on districtwide maintenance and capital construction projects.

6. Assisting the superintendent in an administrative review of the preliminary budget in order to establish priorities.

7. Combination of approved requests into a total receipt-and-expenditure program and preparation of the formal budget document.

8. Assisting the superintendent in the presentation and discussion of the budget with the board of education.

In discharging these responsibilities, the business administrator must exercise care in differentiating between clerical tasks and administrative judgments. Much of the gathering and computing is properly assigned to clerical staff members. However, decisions on format and actual content are administrative and should not be delegated to others.

Annual calendar. The business office should establish a calendar of budget activity so that deadlines can be met without undue exertion. Generally, the annual budget becomes effective before the start of a school year (July 1st is the most common starting date). But business office procedures for preparing the new budget should commence the preceding fall. Here is a generalized calendar of budget activity:

September. The business office prepares and distributes the budget request forms to all schools and departments.

October, November. All staff members assist in identifying budget needs and developing cost estimates for specific proposals. Prime objectives of the total budget are identified and major emphasis in the pattern of expenditures is established at the administrative level. (The development of thoughts for future budgets is a continuous, not a seasonal, activity. However, the plan for the succeeding year should be formally established by October or November.)

December. Budget requests are submitted to central administration. The superintendent presents reports and requests to board of education for major new projects. Each annual budget will have several of these and each should be presented in detail in a setting permitting full consideration, unpressured by deadlines.

January. The business office completes assembly of preliminary budget and forwards it to the superintendent. The superintendent undertakes staff meetings to discuss requirements of individual units and to coordinate these with the total program and resources.

February. Revenue sources, including particularly state financial assistance and local taxes, are analyzed. Final adjustments in preliminary budget are made by the superintendent and his staff. The superintendent prepares his budget message and a letter of transmittal. The business office completes the preparation of the receipts and expenditures, including adjustments made earlier by the superintendent and his staff.

March. The board of education receives the proposed budget, together with budget message.

March, April. The board of education holds a series of meetings to review the superintendent's proposed budget.

April. Lay groups have an opportunity to express opinions on the proposed budget before final board action. In some communities, lay groups participate in development of the preliminary budget. The board of education adopts the budget. A less detailed budget document is prepared and distributed to the public, outlining the educational plans and fiscal needs for the year ahead.

April, May, June. In some school districts, board adoption may be followed by a hearing or vote to ratify the board's decision.

May, June. The business office undertakes the scheduling, ordering, and contracting procedures necessary to insure availability of goods and services at the start of the new fiscal period. Recruitment of additional nonprofessional staff members commences, if such additions are authorized. The nature of the professional job market will require earlier recruitment of personnel to fill these positions.

This is a generalized calendar, designed to illustrate the approximate sequence of budget development. Local regulations and needs would cause some adjustment in the schedule adopted by a particular school district. The salient trait in any sound budget calendar is the provision of ample time for those involved to render thoughtful judgments.

Annual Budget Documents

Capping the budgeting procedures will be the preparation of the budget documents. Normally this will involve two kinds of budgets: a detailed *formal budget* and a *public budget.*

Formal budget. The formal budget should be a specific recitation of facts and figures. It is addressed to a limited audience, generally consisting only of the board of education and the school administration. It serves as a decision-making instrument as the board of education is involved in the adoption process. The same document, as amended, serves as the basis for much of the business office activity during the year to come. It guides a wide range of actions in accounting, purchasing, and staffing.

This budget should outline the program in considerable detail and present supporting data. Since those who work with it will have a direct interest, the possibility of "overburdening" the user is remote. Generally, the more complete the working budget, the simpler it is for the business office to implement its program.

Here is a checklist of the principal components of a sound formal budget:

1. *Table of Contents.*
2. *Superintendent's message.* This includes a statement of educational goals, as well as a review of the current status of the schools and their programs. This should indicate the educational plan for the budget period: what is desired and how it will be achieved. The message should look beyond the immediate budget period and forecast program and expenditure trends over several years. It is worthwhile to include a statement of some of the educationally desirable requests that have been deferred from consideration in the proposed budget.

The message should also identify the cost and character of the significant changes in budget components. These changes may be the result of such factors as increase in enrollments, alterations in class size policies, expansion of course offerings or related services, improvement of salary schedules, or increases in expenditures for supplies and equipment. Frequently, the entire budget increase is explainable on the basis of two or three such conditions, which are repeated through many accounts.

3. *Summary of receipts and expenditures.* A page should be devoted to outlining the major categories of receipts, with a second page for a similar summary treatment of expenditures. This presentation should include some data comparing actual figures for the last full fiscal year with proposed budget figures for present fiscal year. More desirable would be a comparison of data for several years.

4. *Detail of receipts.* This should present an analysis of the sources and kinds of income anticipated during the budget period. Since the number of different kinds of income is limited, this section will not exceed several pages. It should explain, however, how the program is to be financed and should be presented in a complete and accurate fashion.

Comparative figures for the current and previous years should be included.

5. *Summary of expenditures.* This is the bulk of the fiscal budget, and should be developed in detail, with a section allotted to each major account of the state's accounting system. Each section should have a summary, followed by a lucid narration defining the account and analyzing the proposed expenditures. Comparative figures are essential and should cover actual expenses for at least the last full year together with budgeted amounts for the current year and the proposed allocations for the year ahead.

Backing up each sectional summary should be a breakdown of the various subaccounts. This would properly include a line-item description presented in such a manner as to expedite the preparation of accounting records and purchasing and work schedules when the budget year commences.

6. *Statistical data.* This section should consist of a series of tabulations covering a period of at least five years, including the budget year. Useful data include total expenses as well as costs of selected items of expenditure on a per-pupil basis, number of pupils enrolled in each grade, and census figures. The number and assignment of staff members are valuable statistics, as are patterns of revenue, tax rates, and the physical assets of the school district. A table of the district's debt service obligations, projected to maturity, should be included.

Public budget. The public budget is a refined version of the formal budget, prepared for distribution to the public. The general public does not have the deep and technical interest that would warrant distribution of a detailed budget. It is, however, entitled to an explanation of the school's program and a description of its financial support. This justifies preparation of a clear, concise, and attractive document.

Practically all school districts make available some form of budget document to any taxpayer who requests such information. Many school districts undertake a districtwide mailing to all residents, to insure widespread distribution of the proposed budget. This procedure has considerable merit, inasmuch as it does not leave to chance the distribution of information on the public school's program and its finances.

Many school districts include in their public budget a comparison of the local budget with state averages or the budgets of nearby communities. The most frequent comparisons are made among per-pupil expenditures and real estate tax rates. It is logical that many citizens will have a prime concern for these statistics, and they should be made available. Caution must be exercised, however, in drawing conclusions based solely on comparisons of such statistics. Neither of the two sets of figures is, of itself, proof of the presence or absence of quality or economy. This is particularly true of real estate tax rates, which are apt to be related to the amount of property on the tax roll rather than to the expense pattern of the school district.

The use of pictures, diagrams, and charts is a desirable method of presenting certain material. Although figures are essential, they should be general sums. A carefully worded narration should be included to indicate what the budget purports to do for instruction. Although the public document should be made attractive, care must be taken to avoid an ostentatious publication that might generate public concern over extravagance.

In the development of public understanding of the school budget, the standard news media should not be forgotten. These include the daily or weekly newspapers, radio stations, and—in some cases—television stations. These organs of mass communication have an interest in news, and the school program and its finances can indeed be worthy news.

The Capital Expenditure Budget

Although every school district prepares an annual budget, the need for a capital expenditure budget varies among different school systems. Some school districts possess stable pupil populations and modern physical facilities, and they would have little concern with this kind of budgeting. Because of its relatively minor capital needs, a district such as this can include its requirements in its annual budget. Much more typical is the local district that is faced with rapidly expanding enrollments or structures that are nearing the end of their useful life. For these districts, a capital plan is essential.

The magnitude of capital expenditure budgets may be appreciated when it is realized that public school districts in the United States, as mentioned earlier, spend over three billion dollars annually on new school sites, buildings, and equipment. Regardless of the type of district involved, a capital expenditure budget requires many months for identifying needs and planning projects. Expenditures for actual construction usually extend over a period considerably longer than a year.

Planning and budgeting. Planning for extended capital needs will involve projecting enrollments, identifying program offerings, defining space requirements, and establishing revenue forecasts. The outgrowth of this planning will usually be one or more construction or renovation projects. Components of the expenditure plan for large capital expenditures include:

Site purchase	Engineers' fees
Land surveys	Clerk of works' salary
Demolition of buildings	Foundation contract
Bond sale expenses	General construction contract
Legal expenses	Heating and ventilation contract
General administrative costs	Plumbing contract
Architects' fees	Electrical contract
Landscaping contract	Noncontract construction
Sewage contracts	Noncontract building equipment
Water supply contract	Instructional equipment
Walks, roads, and parking areas	Noninstructional equipment
Fences and exterior walls	Playground equipment
Athletic fields and play areas	Builders' risk insurance
Exterior lighting	Performance bonds
Temporary heat	Reserve for contingencies

Financing. There are several ways to finance a capital expenditure budget. One method is for the school district to issue bonds for the project or projects. This permits the cost of the capital improvement to be repaid over an extended period (generally between ten and thirty years). Thus, repayment is made during the prime years of the useful life of the improvement. For districts with substantial immediate needs and limited tax resources, a bond issue makes available the full amount of necessary capital funds.

School district bonds are favored by many investors because the interest earned on these obligations is not subject to federal income tax. Accordingly, schools are able to secure somewhat lower interest rates for a given type of bond than would be available to organizations in private enterprise. It should be recognized that interest charges on long-term bond issues may add as much as 50 per cent or more to the total cost of the improvement. Nevertheless, schools generally have no alternative but to adopt this method of financing their larger capital needs.

A second practice is to establish a reserve fund, and increase this each year by appropriations from the annual budget. When the accumulation within the reserve fund is adequate, the project is undertaken. This procedure is feasible when capital needs are limited and can be anticipated. Another method, practical mainly in very large districts, is to employ annual appropriations for pay-as-you-go capital expenditure budgets.

Long-Range Financial Plan

The intensity of pressure to develop next year's annual budget or a forthcoming building project should not be permitted to obscure concern for long-range financial planning. Just as a school district must have program goals extending far beyond a single year, so must it also forecast revenue and expenditure plans for a period of years. Actually, the need for long-term financial planning flows from the existence of program goals. Since the program goals involve long-term action, so too should the financial planning. As De Young[2] points out, such a plan implies that funds for education are a continuing appropriation, a "fixed charge."

Granted, there is considerable opportunity for error in any long-range plan, regardless of how well qualified the planner may be. It is not unusual for such plans to contain inaccuracies in forecasts of pupil population and omissions of certain elements of supply or equipment. Predictions of salaries and staff positions sometimes go awry. Perhaps the greatest problem is estimating the effect of inflation on the future costs of goods and services.

These pitfalls are avoidable only if extreme care is exercised in the initial planning and if provision is made for periodic revision of forecasts. A long-range plan, developed and kept current under these conditions, is a most valuable chart for the school staff and the board of education. It is an absolute necessity if a school district is to pursue an articulated course over a period of years.

Period of usefulness. The optimum term of a long-range finan-

---

[2] Chris A. De Young, *Budgeting in Public Schools* (Chicago: John S. Swift Co., Inc., 1946), Chap. XV.

cial plan is probably five years. A period of less than five years may not justify the effort required to identify program directions and the establishment of fiscal policies to support them. Conversely, there is some hazard in projecting beyond the five-year mark, because the effect of variables becomes cumulative. Ideally, a school district would seek to establish a plan to cover ten or fifteen years. In practice, this often fails because substantial modification in the emphasis of the instructional program occurs and because drastic changes in the local and national economy may affect enrollments and tax bases.

It is essential that provision for periodic revision be built into the long-range plan. This revision should be done annually, so that the projections reflect the latest intelligence. At the time of this annual revision it is wise to add one year to the plan. This gives the district a continuous long-term plan, always forecast five years in advance but with no estimates over a year old.

Elements. Many of the components of an accurate long-term plan are similar to those found in an annual budget or a capital budget. Frequently the major difference is that it is more essential in long-range forecasting to weigh the effects of time on program, facilities, and finance. Included in the development of a long-range projection should be the following key elements:

Census projections
Nonpublic school plans
Enrollment forecasts
Class size policies
Additional schools
Course offerings
Replacement of older buildings
Major renovation projects
Auxiliary services
Extraclassroom activities
Equipment replacement
Periodic maintenance

Salary schedules
Local tax bases
Assessment practices
State financial assistance
Promotion policies
Grade-level organization
Nonclassroom professional positions
School holding power
Nonprofessional or supporting staff
Fringe benefits
Cost of borrowing money

The business administrator and his office can contribute much to the design and accuracy of the long-range financial plan. His insights into the components of current budgets equip him to participate in

CHAPTER III

School Accounting

Fundamentals

School accounting is the administrative procedure of systematically and completely classifying, recording, reporting, and interpreting the financial transactions of the school district. Its existence is mandated by sound principles of management as well as by law. Accounting is the central activity for most of the functions in the business administration of schools. Rarely can a business assignment be undertaken without involving accounting effort—either the analysis of past records or the creation of new entries.

The casual observer may make the mistake of considering accounting and bookkeeping as synonymous terms. Bookkeeping is the clerical task of entering financial transactions, an essential effort which constitutes only a small component of accounting. Sound accounting is a broader spectrum, consisting also of identifying, designing, analyzing, interpreting, and communicating the fiscal affairs of the school district.

Objectives. A well-designed school accounting operation, integrated with other administrative efforts, will be based on certain generalized objectives. These are concerned with the adequacy of records and their control, analysis, and preservation. The major objectives of school accounting may be delineated as follows:

1. To establish adequate safeguards of public funds by defining responsibility and establishing controls and audit procedures;
2. To furnish a concise and complete permanent record of all financial activity;
3. To establish an expenditure pattern closely related to the adopted budget;
4. To provide a pool of intelligence for the preparation of future budgets and long-range financial plans;

5. To furnish periodic meaningful reports of financial activity for executive and board use in making program decisions;

6. To furnish data for mandatory reports to state and federal agencies;

7. To provide an analysis of fiscal affairs for the public in order to verify that worthy stewardship has been rendered;

8. To provide documentation of compliance with mandates imposed by law.

Rules of action. Public school accounting has been sufficiently refined for the competent observer to distill a series of general rules of action. Although these are not immutable, they represent what is presently thought to be sound practice. Among the major rules of action are the following:

1. The accounting procedures should comply with the requirements of state law and regulation.

2. Financial records should be kept current by prompt recording of transactions, including an encumbering procedure for outstanding obligations.

3. The accounting procedures should produce facts that reflect the actual financial condition of the school district.

4. A common and consistent classification should interlace the budget, the accounting function, and the reporting function.

5. The design of the accounting function should be closely oriented to local management needs.

6. Provision should be made for periodic analysis of methods, funds, and classifications, to insure maintenance of flexibility and adaptability.

7. Accounting procedures should include provision for internal controls.

8. The managerial responsibility for all school district funds should be centralized under one accounting officer, typically the school business administrator.

9. The disbursement of funds should be a responsibility shared by two or more persons, with separation of the authorization and issuance procedures.

10. Adequate safeguards should be maintained to preserve accounting records against loss or damage.

11. The accounting process should provide for a control on receipts and expenditures, to assure adherence to the budget.

12. Provision should be made for the periodic inventory of all properties of the district.

13. Monthly financial reports should be rendered to the board of education.

14. An independent audit of all school district financial records should be conducted annually.

It should be realized that accounting is more of an art than a science and that the art is frequently restricted by the environment in which it is practiced. State laws or regulations usually define much of the method, format, and scope of financial record keeping. Although there are accounting principles that might possess intrinsic validity in all school situations, their application in a particular district may conflict with legal requirements. In such circumstances the law must be complied with, even if the accounting principles are compromised or negated.

Furthermore, there is no single system of accounting that can be superior for every school system. Such a standard scheme would be too complex and costly in some cases and inadequate in others. The size, kind, and location of the school district, the size of its administrative or business office, and the perceptions and standards of its board of education, administration, and patrons will all contribute to the determination of what is most effective.

Funds and accounts. The basic entity in school accounting is a fund which may be defined as a resource set aside for a particular purpose. In this context the word *resource* includes more than cash; it also includes the district's assets (land, buildings, buses, equipment, taxes receivable, and state aid receivable) plus contingent assets (income from tuition payments, rental for use of facilities, and similar charges). However, the major concern is with the receipt and disbursement of cash.

The kinds of funds that a school district may establish are generally specified by the state. The most important, common to all school districts, is the general fund. This fund should cover substantially all the common and continuing activities of school district fiscal operation. It has its basis in the school budget, which identifies both anticipated receipts and estimated expenditures. Other frequently used funds include building, cafeteria, retirement and pension, sinking, trust, revolving, student activity, and contingency funds.

Careful classification will usually make it possible to achieve satisfactory results with no more than two or three funds. It is advisable to keep the number of funds to the minimum consistent with managerial and legal requirements, thereby reducing the amount of accounting effort.

Cash versus accrual basis. The basis on which a receipt or expenditure is recognized and the appropriate accounting entry made is a subject of continuing debate among school business administrators. One school of opinion adheres to the *cash basis;* the other, to the *accrual basis.*

The cash basis is quite simple and involves merely listing receipts and expenditures at the time they actually occur. The cash basis, as Tidwell indicates, "is inherently incapable of recording completely and reporting fully the nature and the results of all business transactions." [1] A prime example of this occurs in relation to the obligations for goods and services contracted for, but not yet paid for. Even though large sums may be involved, these transactions are not recognized until the disbursing check is drawn.

The accrual basis makes the accounting entry at the time the revenue is earned or the expenditure liability is incurred. Thus, the cost of goods and services would be charged to expenditures at the time the purchase order or contract is issued. The accrual basis is acknowledged to be a more accurate method involving greater effort and is recommended, where applicable, by the National Committee on Governmental Accounting. However, the accounting and reporting regulations of many states do not make this method feasible.

The best current practice is to handle school accounting on a modified basis. A common modification is to treat all receipts on a cash basis and to record most or all expenditures on an accrual basis. Another alteration is to encumber expenditure appropriations at the time charges for goods and services are incurred. Encumbering reserves a portion of the total appropriation, ample to accommodate the actual expenditure, although the latter is not posted until the check is drawn.

---

[1] Sam B. Tidwell, *Public School Fund Accounting* (New York: Harper & Row, Publishers, 1960), p. 8.

General Fund Receipts

Receipts and *revenues* are not interchangeable terms, although revenues are a part of receipts. Incoming school district monies will consist of two kinds of receipts: revenue and nonrevenue. Revenue receipts increase assets without increasing the outstanding debt or reducing the worth of the property. State financial aid and local taxes are common examples. Nonrevenue receipts result from incurring an obligation or reducing property worth. Proceeds of building bonds constitute a nonrevenue receipt.

In the operation of the general fund, the school district is concerned principally with revenue receipts, since these constitute the great bulk of the operating income. However, it is essential that the accounting records also identify the nonrevenue receipts. Proceeds from bond sales are usually maintained in a separate construction fund. Proceeds from sales of property are insignificant in amount except when a building is disposed of, but these should be recorded as nonrevenue receipts. Amounts received from other districts for education or transportation service are nonrevenue items, as are loans. For those loans made and repaid during the same fiscal period, it is satisfactory to make a memorandum entry in the accounting records.

Local taxation. About 55 per cent of all school district revenues in the United States arise from local taxation. Taxes are compulsory charges levied by a governmental unit for the purpose of financing services performed for the common benefit. Usually taxes for school purposes are levied by the board of education. However, in a minority of cases the board of education requests or specifies a sum, but the actual levy is made by another agency of local government.

Property taxes constitute about 95 per cent of all local school district taxes. Property taxes are levied on a tax roll listing all the assessable properties within the district. Usually the school district receives the tax roll from another source—the city, town, township, or county—which prepares one master roll for several different local levies. This method is usually advantageous to the school district, saving effort and expense.

The actual collection of school taxes is frequently a function performed by the school district. Larger school districts, particularly those in cities, are more apt to have the municipality handle tax collection and deposit the proceeds to the school fund. Even when a fee is charged for this collection, it is generally acknowledged that the municipality can prepare, issue, and collect tax bills more efficiently than the school district can.

Nonproperty taxes, which constitute the other 5 per cent of local taxation, are increasing in kind and value, although only a minority of districts levy them. These include taxes on retail sales, utility bills, motor vehicles, payrolls, alcoholic beverages, admissions, hotel rooms, vending machines, and horseracing. Such taxes are sometimes levied by the school district; in other cases the town, township, county, or city levies the tax and the school receives all or a portion of the yield.

State financial assistance. This comprises about 40 per cent of local district revenue. Most state aid results from legislative appropriations, although some income arises from permanent school endowment funds of the state. Over half of the dollar value of state assistance is now distributed on an "equalized" basis: the district with less than the average local tax base receives a proportionately higher amount of state assistance than a more wealthy district. Most of the balance of state aid is distributed as a "flat grant," an allocation based on the number of pupils, teachers, classrooms, or schools in a given district. A relatively small amount of aid is earmarked for special programs, usually on a flat grant basis.

Federal assistance. Comprising about 4 per cent of all local revenue, federal aid to the general fund consists mainly of grants for special educational programs or for assistance in erecting and operating schools in areas with large government-owned properties. Although the average district receives little federal aid, those closely associated with national defense installations receive a significant portion of their revenue from this source.

Other local income. This represents a very small percentage of total local revenues. Such income would arise from a variety of sources: tuition charges from nonresidents, adult education fees, rentals, gifts, various fines, sale of obsolete material, service charges, and earnings from temporary investments or deposits.

Handling of receipts. State regulations generally mandate the procedure for handling and recording receipts. At least one record of income should be maintained, in which the receipts are analyzed in detail as to date, source, amount, and type. Some districts follow the sound practice of maintaining a cash book as a second record. The cash book may be more brief, showing only the date, source, receipt number, and amount of each transaction.

Among the better practices for safeguarding receipts are the following:

1. A press-numbered treasurer's receipt is issued for all receipts.
2. The treasurer and all personnel responsible for the handling of receipts are covered by surety bonds.
3. Where possible, the school district's bank account is guaranteed or bonded.
4. Deposits to the bank account are made promptly.
5. Bank statements are reconciled monthly.
6. Monthly reports of receipts are submitted to the board of education.
7. An annual external audit is conducted.

General Fund Expenditures

General fund expenditure accounting centers about three main processes: (1) the payment of staff members for personal services; (2) the payment of vendors for goods and services; and (3) the recording of these transactions in a manner that provides essential controls and needed information. The starting point and the control of general fund expenditure accounting is the adopted budget. This cites the appropriations for each of the accounts and subaccounts of expenditure.

Payroll accounting. Measured either by volume of expenditures or by volume of activity, payroll accounting comprises the major portion of general fund expenditures. Direct and indirect payroll expenditures usually consume 80–90 per cent of the school district's operating costs. Depending on frequency of payment, between two thirds and three fourths of the total number of checks issued by the district will be for payroll purposes.

The tremendous growth in salary options and payroll deductions has made payroll accounting a complex routine. Payments for professional staff members are generally made once or twice a month.

These payments may be made for nine or ten months, or on a twelve-months' basis. Supporting or noninstructional staff members may receive their paychecks once a week, every second week, twice a month, or once a month. Further complicating the compensation of supporting staff members may be a difference in work year, with some members employed for the school year, others for the full twelve months.

Payroll deductions include those mandated by law and those made for optional fringe benefits. Many of the fringe benefits involve joint contributions from the school district and from the individual employee. Among the more common deductions are those for:

Income tax	Life insurance	Teachers Association
Pension	Savings bonds	dues
Social Security	Credit Union	Union dues
Health insurance		Community fund

No matter which accounting system is used, two important accounting records should be maintained in the payroll operation: a payroll journal and an individual earnings record. At the time the individual paycheck is prepared, all pertinent data should be recorded on both of these valuable records.

The individual earnings record is a separate accounting record which contains cumulative payroll information for each individual. It covers the full fiscal period, with an entry made each time a paycheck is drawn for the employee. It provides an analysis of payments to the individual and assists in preparation of reports for Social Security, retirement systems, withholding tax, and similar purposes.

Payroll checks should have a detachable stub describing the pay period, any adjustments, the amount of gross earnings, the kind and amount of payroll deductions, and the net earnings (the face amount of the paycheck).

Because of the great amount of money involved and because these checks are drawn to individuals, extreme care must be exercised in all payroll accounting activity. Since most payroll entries are largely repetitive and continuous, there is an ever-present hazard of a slackening of controls.

There are three distinct aspects in the compensation of school district staff members:

1. Appointment to the position and establishment of salary;
2. Verification of the rendering of service;
3. Preparation and distribution of the paycheck.

The formal appointment of staff members is by action of the board of education, ordinarily subsequent to a recommendation of the superintendent of schools. The appointment should specify a salary according to the salary schedule adopted by the board of education. The verification of the rendering of service is an administrative task that is normally assigned to the building principal or other supervisor. Payroll preparation should be separate and distinct from appointment and verification. Such a separation of authority and responsibility for compensation makes it unlikely that impropriety can arise. Further insurance against such a danger is obtained by providing sound payroll audit procedures.

Payment of vendors. Payments to vendors are made in return for a wide variety of goods and services purchased by the school district. There are periods of peak activity—for instance, the start of a new school year—but most districts process a substantial number of payments each month throughout the year.

School districts usually pay vendors' claims only after these have been formally approved by the board of education. Frequently boards hold but one formal meeting each month. Thus, intensive preparation immediately in advance of the meeting date is necessary. Some school districts are permitted by law to pay vendors' claims continuously, on the basis of an audit by an administrative staff member. The advantages of such a plan include a more even distribution of the accounting workload throughout the entire month, the possibility of taking cash discounts for prompt payment of claims, and an improved relationship with vendors because of the rapidity with which claims are processed.

The vendor's claim is the originating instrument for all accounts payable activity. In some cases the vendor merely submits his standard invoice in support of the claim. A large number of school districts require the submission of a claim form, the contents of which are usually mandated by state regulation.

The claim form usually requests standard billing data, plus an affidavit or certification by the vendor that (a) he has rendered the services or delivered the material included in the claim, (b) that the charges are just and proper, and (c) that payment has not been made to date. The advantages of a claim form are that it provides a certification and is standardized in size and contents. Partially offsetting these advantages is the extra burden it imposes on the billing operation of some vendors.

Normally the extensions of prices listed in the claim are checked and receipt of goods is verified. Verification is best made by securing a signed receiving copy of the purchase order originally written to authorize the purchase. The signature of the proper school staff member on the receiving copy acknowledges delivery of the specified material or service. A check may then be prepared. (In practice several claim forms from a single vendor may be combined for payment with one check.) A portion of the check should contain a remittance advice, indicating the claims for which payment is being made.

At the same time these checks are drawn, a check register is prepared. This lists each check serially and records significant elements, such as the date, name of payee, amount, budgetary code, and claim form number. The check, or a copy, is then used to charge the particular accounts benefiting by the transaction. In manual accounting this would usually require hand-posting to several columnar forms. A different form is used for each major account, such as instructional services and maintenance of plant. A separate column is allotted to each subaccount in the major account. Machine accounting typically utilizes a separate ledger card for each subaccount.

Internal control should be exerted most strongly at two locations in the accounts payable process. First, the receipt of the goods or services should be verified by a responsible staff member. This should not be a person who is involved in preparing the check for payment. Second, the claim should be verified for accuracy in quantity, price, price extension, and absence of prior payment.

Encumbrances. Encumbrances are outstanding commitments of the school district which are known to exist and are chargeable against a budgetary appropriation. Under the cash system of accounting followed by the majority of smaller school districts, these commitments are not discernible in the accounting records. The only posting of such a commitment under this system occurs when the claim is paid—perhaps months after the obligation was incurred. Furthermore, lack of knowledge of the nature and amount of outstanding commitments may give a misleading image of the status of budgetary appropriations. Because a certain account has a substantial cash balance on a given date does not mean that additional orders may be placed and charged against the account. In fact, the account may have outstanding charges that completely offset the cash balance.

To overcome this hazard, a system of encumbering or balance earmarking has been devised. Each time an obligation is incurred, the balance of the appropriate account is encumbered for the estimated cost of the transaction. In effect, this reserves a portion of the cash allowance to pay for this obligation when the bill is presented. When payment is actually made, the encumbrance is liquidated. Sometimes the final payment differs slightly from the encumbered sum because of price changes or shipping charges. In such cases, the amount of encumbrances outstanding is reduced only by the amount of the original encumbrance. The check, of course, is drawn in the correct amount of the final bill and the full charge is recorded as an expenditure.

Regardless of whether manual methods or machine methods are used for the accounting process, it is possible to revise present procedures to include the encumbrance technique. Added clerical effort and several additional columns for the posting of encumbrance data are required.

Some school districts record encumbrances only in supply and equipment accounts, where the number of outstanding commitments is frequently large and easily ignored. However, other districts extend the encumbering procedure to all appropriations. In this event the following items would be utilized for establishing the encumbrances:

1. Purchase orders, as they are written;
2. Purchase and service contracts, as they are awarded;
3. Salaries, as designated by board of education action;

4. Fuel and utilities, as estimated;
5. Debt service, as established by the bond schedules.

Encumbering of expenditure records is an excellent method of maintaining budgetary control. It removes the major shortcoming of cash accounting by bringing appropriation balances up to date. Yet it is not as complex as the accrual basis of accounting favored in private business and industry.

Classification

Classification is the system of grouping accounting entries to provide a consistent basis for interpretation. There are at least six acceptable methods of classifying public school receipts and expenditures:

1. Function	4. Activity
2. Character	5. Unit
3. Object	6. Fund

Since receipts are relatively few in number and kind, they present little difficulty in classification. The major complication is in classifying expenditures, which involves differentiating between function, character, and object.

The pioneer work of Hiram C. Case prior to World War I resulted in a handbook [2] that became the national guide for school accounting. This handbook developed a system for classifying receipts and expenditures that has become the standard in the field. Many states still utilize this system, although with minor modifications. Expenditures are divided into eight major accounts:

1. General control (administration)	5. Fixed charges
	6. Auxiliary agencies
2. Instructional services	7. Debt service
3. Plant operation	8. Capital outlay
4. Plant maintenance	

These major accounts were designed on the basis of the function and character of the expenditure. Subaccounts under these major accounts catalog the objects involved in expenditures.

---

[2] Hiram C. Case, *Handbook of Instructions for Recording Disbursements for School Purposes* (Albany, N.Y.: C. F. Williams and Sons, Inc., 1916).

After the system had been in use for forty years, some of its limitations gave rise to an interest in revising the uniform classifications. In 1957, the U.S. Office of Education issued a handbook [3] which recommended a new national standard of accounting classification. The handbook contained the findings of a series of conferences, held over a three-year period and attended by representatives of the major professional organizations.

The table on pages 42 and 43 was taken from the handbook. It summarizes the recommended receipts and expenditure classifications.

The proposed new system of expenditure classification includes twelve accounts in place of the eight used by Case. The principal area of change is in those services that have expanded rapidly in recent years. For example, Attendance and Health Services is now a separate account. Attendance costs had usually been included in General Control, and health services were considered part of the Auxiliary Agencies account.

Pupil Transportation Services is another new account, as are Food Services, Student-Body Activities, and Community Services. In the Case system, these were usually considered part of Auxiliary Agencies expenditures.

The purpose of the new national handbook is to facilitate uniformity in local and state accounting standards and terminology. The hope is that a new national standard, refined and implemented in state and local situations, would make possible improvements in these activities:

Budgeting	Reporting
Cost accounting	Comparison studies
Accounting processes	Research

This new scheme is being adopted, but at a slow pace. This is understandable, because alteration of school district accounting classifications usually requires modification of state regulations, manuals, reports, and practices.

---

[3] Paul L. Reason and Alpheus L. White, *Financial Accounting for Local and State School Systems, Standard Receipts and Expenditure Accounts,* U.S. Office of Education Bulletin 1957, No. 4 (Washington, D.C.: USGPO, 1957).

TABLE I

Outline of Basic Accounts [4]

RECEIPT ACCOUNTS

Revenue Receipts
10–40 Series

10. Revenue from Local Sources
  11. Taxation and Appropriations Received
  12. Tuition from Patrons
  13. Transportation Fees from Patrons
  14. Other Revenue from Local Sources
20. Revenue from Intermediate Sources
30. Revenue from State Sources
40. Revenue from Federal Sources

Nonrevenue Receipts
50–70 Series

50. Sale of Bonds
60. Loans
70. Sale of School Property and Insurance Adjustments

Incoming Transfer Accounts
80–90 Series

80. Amounts Received from Other School Districts in State
90. Amounts Received from School Districts in Another State

EXPENDITURE ACCOUNTS

Administration
100 Series

110. Salaries
120. Contracted Services
130. Other Expenses

Instruction
200 Series

210. Salaries
  211. Principals
  212. Consultants or Supervisors
  213. Teachers
  214. Other Instructional Staff
  215. Secretarial and Clerical Assistants
216. Other Salaries for Instruction

Attendance and Health Services
300–400 Series

300. Attendane Services
  310. Salaries
  320. Other Expenses
400. Health Services
  410. Salaries
  420. Other Expenses

Pupil Transportation Services
500 Series

510. Salaries
520. Contracted Service and Public Carriers
530. Replacements of Vehicles
540. Transportation Insurance
550. Expenditures in Lieu of Transportation
560. Other Expenses

Maintenance of Plant
700 Series

710. Salaries
720. Contracted Services
730. Replacements of Equipment
740. Other Expenses

Fixed Charges
800 Series

810. Employee Retirement
820. Insurance and Judgments
830. Rental of Land and Buildings
840. Interest on Current Loans
850. Other Fixed Charges

220. Textbooks
230. School Libraries and Audiovisual
240. Teaching Supplies
250. Other Expenses

Food Services and Student-Body Activities
900–1000 Series

900. Food Services
910. Salaries
920. Other Expenses
930. Separate Fund or Account
1000. Student-Body Activities
1001. Salaries
1020. Other Expenses
1030. Separate Fund or Account

Community Services
1100 Series

1110. Recreation
1120. Civic Activities
1130. Public Libraries
1140. Custodial and Detention Care of Children
1150. Welfare Activities
1160. Nonpublic school Pupils
1161. Instructional Services
1162. Attendance and Health Services
1163. Transportation Services

Operation of Plant
600 Series

610. Salaries
620. Contracted Services
630. Heat for Buildings
640. Utilities, Except Heat
650. Supplies
660. Other Expenses

Capital Outlay
1200 Series

1210. Sites
1220. Buildings
1230. Equipment

Debt Service from Current Funds
1300 Series

1310. Principal of Debt
1320. Interest on Debt
1330. Paid into Sinking Funds
1340. Schoolhousing Authority
1350. Other Debt Service

Outgoing Transfer Accounts
1400 Series

1410. Districts in the State
1420. Districts in Another State
1430. Tuition to Other Than Public Schools

4 *Ibid.*, pp. xviii–xix.

Machine Accounting

Machine accounting is the utilization of mechanical equipment to process part or all of the school district's accounting activity. The equipment available ranges from a simple adding machine to a highly complicated data-processing complex. Several other mechanical systems lie between these two extremes of capacity, price, and performance.

This range of available machines brings the basic issue of machine accounting into sharp focus. The question is usually not: "Should our school have machine accounting?" The answer to this is usually affirmative. Rather, the question is: "What type of equipment should we use for our accounting operation?" The response to this is involved because of differences in the size and complexity of school systems and because of the broad range of function, capacity, cost, and manpower requirements found in different machines.

Types of accounting machines. It is doubtful that a school district with fewer than 1500–2000 pupils should have any accounting machine more complicated than a listing machine. Larger districts may choose one of three principal varieties of equipment:

Nondescriptive accounting machine. This is a big, elaborate adding machine that prints and accumulates several different columns of figures and can be used for payroll preparation as well as for appropriation accounting. It will print only figures, not letters. A second device must be employed for printing names of vendors or employees and similar information. This may be done with a typewriter or an addressing machine using stencils or plates. The limitation of this equipment is that two separate operations are required for many tasks.

Descriptive accounting machine. This unit has all the features of the nondescriptive accounting machine, plus a typewriter keyboard which may be used for typing all descriptive data as well as for recording figure amounts on voucher checks, payroll checks, and related journals. Thus, the unit may be utilized to do a total job of accounting, except for computing.

Data-processing equipment. This equipment can be designed to compute as well as to prepare financial records. If a computer is included, the complex will compute the earnings, withhold appropriate sums for taxes and other deductions, draw a net paycheck, and post all subsidiary payroll records. Similar complete computation and preparation operations can be utilized in ordering, paying vendors' claims, preparing financial reports, and making detailed cost studies. The potential of these complexes is limited mainly by the imagination of the programmer.

They will produce, in moments, analyses that would take weeks to produce with less sophisticated equipment.

The major barrier to exploitation of data-processing units by school districts is their cost. Present equipment can be justified on economic grounds only in very large school districts. Sophisticated equipment, oriented about a computer, is of doubtful economy for business operations in school districts with fewer than 50,000 pupils. Less complicated equipment is of marginal value in school districts with fewer than 20,000 pupils unless a large number of nonfinancial operations are assigned to the complex. By additional utilization of such equipment in nonbusiness functions, some smaller districts can justify the expense. The future will undoubtedly see the development of less costly data-processing equipment. When this occurs, the investment will be justified in medium-sized districts.

Criteria for selection. Most school districts with over approximately 2000 pupils can justify a machine installation on the basis of function and savings. The type that will best serve a particular district is determined by the responses to such questions as:

1. Does the equipment have ample flexibility for future changes in function and work load?
2. What is the reasonable useful life of the unit or complex?
3. Will the proposed equipment be more efficient than the present method?
4. Can and should the equipment be utilized for nonfinancial accounting operations?
5. What will be the cost of forms and supplies?
6. How accessible are parts and service and what will these cost?
7. How much space is required for the installation of the equipment?
8. How much staff will be required to operate the equipment?
9. How much skill, training, and experience will be required of this staff?
10. What will be the net cost of the new equipment and its operation?
11. Is the equipment available for prompt delivery?

Student Activity Funds

Student activity funds consist of money or other resources which belong to student groups but remain in the custody of the school district. The expansion of activity programs has caused activity funds to increase to major proportions in volume and complexity. Many such funds in medium-sized secondary schools approach $100,000 in annual expenditures.

Responsibility. Usually by statute, sometimes by custom, the board of education is given the responsibility for the sound management of student activity funds. In discharging this obligation, the board of education should adopt rules which establish careful and complete accounting for these funds.

Student activity funds are unique in school financial activity. True, they may be defined as trust funds of the board of education; but, more important, they are a source of learning for the boys and girls of the school. Because of the involvement of pupils, some activity fund accounting procedures may seem cumbersome and inefficient. But these are, hopefully, affording priceless learnings to youngsters.

In most school districts the student activity funds are maintained in the individual school buildings and are the administrative responsibility of the building principal. In some large districts, control and management may be centralized, usually in the district business office. Most educators agree that the direct management of these funds should be the responsibility of the building principal. The role of the central office should be principally to design activity fund accounting procedures and to arrange for systematic reports and annual audits.

Procedures. It is impossible to describe a system of accounting for student activity funds that will have universal application. First, the nature of school staffs and activity programs varies widely. Second, many states have adopted regulations that detail the procedures for activity fund accounting. The following is a generalized description of a well-organized accounting operation, involving four key positions:

1. *Central treasurer* (faculty member). This officer has custody of all monies, receiving them from student treasurers, issuing receipts, and depositing them in a bank account. He makes expenditures on the basis of checks drawn and countersigned by the central controller. He records all receipts and payments in a cash book, prepares a monthly report, and reconciles the monthly bank statement.

2. *Central controller* (faculty member). This officer audits each receipt and expenditure and maintains budgetary control over individual activities. He approves each expenditure for payment by preparing and signing the check. He maintains a receipts and expenditures ledger for each activity.

3. *Student treasurer* (student). Each activity has a student treasurer who receives the money collected in the activity and transmits it to the central treasurer for deposit. He prepares and signs a disbursing order for each authorized payment and forwards it to the activity advisor. He approves all invoices related to his activity, maintains a record of activity receipts and disbursements, and submits regular financial reports to his activity.

4. *Activity advisor* (faculty member). Each activity has an activity advisor who assists and guides the students. He approves all requisitions and disburses orders and invoices related to his activity. He oversees the student treasurer in maintaining adequate records.

The foregoing system assumes a single fund to cover all student activities. This method is usually favored because it simplifies accounting and control, although some schools maintain separate funds for each activity. Some schools dispense with the accounting records maintained by the central controller and increase the detail of the central treasurer's records.

Guidelines. There are some general guidelines to sound management of student activity funds:

1. Two separate sets of accounting records should be maintained, at least one by a faculty member.

2. The authority to expend funds should be distinct from the custody of the funds.

3. Press-numbered receipts should be issued for all money received.

4. All incoming money should be deposited in the bank by the central treasurer.

5. Payment of all expenditures should be requested by submission of a disbursing order.

6. All expenditures should be made by check, signed by two faculty members.

7. A budget should be established for each activity and budgetary controls exercised on expenditures.

8. Bank statements should be reconciled monthly.

9. Fidelity bonds should be secured for faculty participants.

10. An external audit should be performed annually.

11. A monthly report, including a statement of the receipts, disbursements, and balances for each activity, should be submitted by the central treasurer.

Auditing

Auditing is the critical analysis of the financial transactions of the school district to insure compliance with state laws and standards. It is one of the most significant prudential controls of school district operations. For the public, it provides assurance that school funds are being used properly. For the school business staff, a successful audit is a vote of confidence for worthy stewardship of financial matters.

Internal audits. As the name implies, internal audits are performed from within the school system by an employee or employees of the district. Internal audits are generally conducted continuously over the entire year. Auditing personnel are engaged in viewing fiscal activity on a pre-audit or recent-review basis.

Internal auditing is most apt to exist in larger school districts, where volume and complexity justify the staff required. Typical among items of concern in internal audits are collection and deposit procedures for receipts, safeguarding of funds practices, budgetary control, purchase order writing, and awarding of bids. Also, the accuracy of deliveries—both as to quality and quantity—is verified, payroll procedures are reviewed, vendors' claims are analyzed, and accounts payable are processed.

The school district not large enough to support a full-time auditing staff can still avail itself of a pre-audit by devising internal controls. These controls can be shared by one or more persons who have other primary duties. Ideally, the primary duties should be unrelated to the control assignment.

Post-audits. Post-audits are the review of fiscal affairs after the completion of the period. This may be conducted by a committee appointed by the board of education, by state auditors, or by independent auditors. The movement has been away from committee audits because these tend to be superficial.

State audits frequently extend beyond the verification of the accuracy of accounting transactions to an examination of whether or not the transaction was authorized by existing law or regulation. One disadvantage of many state-conducted audits is that they are not annual; two or three years may elapse between examinations. An annual review, conducted immediately after the close of the fiscal year, is desirable because it makes possible the prompt correction of any procedures found wanting.

The ideal post-audit is an annual examination of financial affairs by an independent auditing firm. The firm should be selected by the board of education with the same care applied to the selection of any other professional service. Not only should the firm possess a fine general reputation, it should also have some knowledge and experience in public school district auditing.

The audit report. It is most important that the results of post-audits be addressed directly to the board of education. Under no circumstances should the auditor report to an administrative staff member. To do this would be to jeopardize the very purpose of auditing.

The contents of the audit report of public accountants should conform to the three-section report format recommended by the National Committee on Governmental Accounting:

1. A letter of transmittal indicating the scope and limitations of the audit, the findings of the audit, the recommendations of changes in accounting procedure and the auditor's opinion.
2. A financial section detailing the position and activity of the school district funds during the audit period.
3. A statistical section presenting appropriate tables of business activity related to the funds being audited. This material can be both analytical and informational.

Cost Analysis

The need. The alert administrator will frequently want to know what a particular element of the educational program costs. As

Mort, Reusser, and Polley [5] state: "Accurate analysis of cost is essential to effective control of the educational enterprise. . . ."

Technically, cost comprises more than current out-of-pocket expenditures. Cost accountants may work with over a score of different types of costs. However, in public school accounting, it is general practice to accept the actual expenditure as being the basis of cost.

Public school expenses are usually analyzed in one or more of the following categories:

Total
Current
Net current
Instructional Supplies and Materials

Operation of plant
Instructional
Transportation

Maintenance of plant
Administration
Construction

Pupil units. Costs may be analyzed in a wide variety of units of measurement—among them, pupils, teachers, mileage, and square feet. However, for purposes of this discussion, the basic unit of analysis will be cost per pupil for a school year.

The pupil unit may vary in two dimensions:

1. *Grade-level of pupils.* The grade-level may be a particular grade (such as half-day kindergarten) or a group of grades (such as elementary, junior, or senior high school).

2. *Attendance.* The standard unit of measurement has been A.D.A., or average daily attendance. A refinement of this measure is W.A.D.A., or weighted average daily attendance. This measure applies a downward correction for half-day kindergarten pupils and an upward correction for secondary school pupils and is designed to reflect the differences in instruction costs between these two extremes and the standard unit of elementary pupils in full-day session. The U.S. Office of Education [6] suggests using average daily membership as the unit of measurement because it averages out the pupil load that the school is responsible for instructing, even though some of this group may be temporarily absent.

Prorating. Many items of expenditure cover goods or services utilized in more than one area of operation. For example, gasoline

---

[5] Paul R. Mort, Walter C. Reusser, and John W. Polley, *Public School Finance* (New York: McGraw-Hill, Inc., 1960), Chap. 20.

[6] Paul L. Reason and Alpheus L. White, *Financial Accounting for Local and State School Systems, Standard Receipt and Expenditure Accounts,* U.S. Office of Education Bulletin 1957, No. 4 (Washington, D.C.: USGPO, 1957).

may be used for pupil transportation, for operation of driver-education cars, and for operation of maintenance vehicles. This fact should be recognized by prorating the total cost among the elements receiving the benefit. The state coding system generally furnishes a standard for proration, as does the U.S. Office of Education *Handbook on Financial Accounting for Local and State School Systems.*

Financial Reporting

Financial reporting is the meaningful portrayal of the details of the accounting transactions in a school district for a given period of time. Since the source for this report is the accounting records, it follows that the design features of the accounting system should include recognition of the reporting function. The accounting records should be organized so that report data is easily extracted.

Reports to staff and board of education. Financial reports to the staff and the board of education require the greatest effort because they are frequent and detailed. Normally, this material will be presented in written form, although the possibility of an oral presentation should not be overlooked. In some instances, a brief oral presentation, followed by a question-and-answer period, provides a more complete understanding of the financial picture with less effort for all.

An ideal report would meet these criteria:

1. It should be written and distributed monthly.
2. It should be sent to board members several days before a board meeting.
3. It should be included on the meeting agenda.
4. It should become a part of the formal minutes.
5. It should contain a brief narrative summary, and a detailed tabulation of receipts and expenditures.
6. It should compare the current status with the year to date and the similar period of the previous year.
7. It should contain a closing balance, reconciled to a bank statement.

Reports to public. Financial reporting should be an integral part of the interpretive material distributed to the public. Such reporting should be made on a regular basis, the most advantageous time probably being at the close of the fiscal year. The most frequently used medium for reporting is the local newspaper. However, many school districts follow the practice of including the financial report in an issue of a school-to-community publication.

Care in the selection and presentation of appropriate material is a major problem in public reports. The format that is meaningful in a report for administrative staff and board of education personnel may be completely unsatisfactory for the lay public. A financial report to the public should be factual, interesting, simple, clear, and reasonably brief.

State, federal, and professional reports. State and federal reports generally require detailed financial and statistical information. State reports usually request that data be presented in the same format as it is presented in the state accounting system. This enables the local administrator to establish his accounts in a manner that will facilitate completion of these reports.

Professional reports may be either periodic (usually on an annual basis) or nonrepeating. The organizations involved are wisely developing their timetable and format for annual reports to accommodate existing state reports. This results in a considerable reduction in the amount of effort required for preparation. Presumably it also results in a greater response, thus making the results more valid.

CHAPTER IV

Purchasing

Principles of Purchasing

Purchasing is the integrated procedure of selecting, ordering, and acquiring the supplies and equipment necessary for support of the school program. To indicate that it includes considerably more than buying, the total process is frequently called *procurement*. Most school districts will expend between 10 and 20 per cent of their annual budgets in obtaining these materials.

It is true that school district purchasing does not involve as great a percentage of total expenditures as this function would in other enterprises. For example, a manufacturing firm might find that 50–75 per cent of its total expenses are for purchases. Schools are basically service institutions; thus, the major portion of costs is for salaries. This is not to indicate that school district purchasing is not a large-scale effort. The nation's schools expend several billions of dollars annually and purchase a large volume of widely diversified products. The purchasing responsibility was concisely defined by Heinritz,[1] as "buying materials of the right quality, in the right quantity, at the right time, at the right price, from the right source."

The principles of purchasing are the same for all school districts, although operational procedures may vary from one district to another. Methods and procedures should differ as a function of the size or type of school district. But procuring mimeograph paper, for example, whether for a small rural district or a large city district, involves the same basic considerations.

Legal requirements. Purchasing, like most other activities of school districts, is governed by state law and local policy. Boards of education are creatures of the state and have only such powers as are explicitly granted by statute or as may be reasonably implied

---

[1] Stuart F. Heinritz, *Purchasing,* 2nd ed. (Englewood Cliffs, N.J.: Prentice-Hall, Inc., 1951), p. 13.

from it. Generally speaking, these laws and policies are considerably more specific and more restrictive than the rules that govern purchasing by private organizations.

The school district usually has complete freedom to make purchase commitments (within the confines of statute and the limits of budgetary appropriations). In some cities, however, the purchasing of goods and services for schools is a municipal function. Even so, the school district has considerable responsibility in the procurement of materials, such as identifying the kinds and quantities of supplies and equipment required and storing and distributing these materials after delivery.

Typically, state law will include the purchasing of essential goods among the specific responsibilities of the local board of education. Usually the state law will not define purchasing as an administrative function. This means that in many cases the administrative staff member who is designated to make purchases performs this role solely on the basis of local board delegation.

It is accepted as a matter of law that boards of education can delegate only those functions which they are authorized by statute to delegate. The prudent board of education will designate a purchasing agent, but confine his actions to those that may be discharged by an employee. Depending on the statute, this may mean that the board either ratifies individual actions of the purchasing agent or reserves to itself the privilege of awarding the larger purchase contracts. This does not diminish the responsibility of the purchasing agent to exercise sound judgment in selecting materials, obtaining prices or bids, and preparing recommendations.

The purchasing agent. The use of the word *agent* in the title of the school purchasing official is significant, for an agent is one who acts for or represents a principal in a transaction with a third party. This title precisely identifies the relationship and authority of the administrator appointed by the board of education to oversee purchasing.

In a smaller school district, the superintendent of schools would be the purchasing agent. Districts of medium size usually include this assignment among the responsibilities of the assistant superintendent for business or the business manager. Large districts with a purchasing department frequently employ a full-time purchasing agent.

Regardless of his title, a school district's purchasing agent

1. Seeks to standardize materials as far as is practical;
2. Maintains a list of sources for materials;
3. Prepares and maintains specifications;
4. Issues purchase orders;
5. Secures quotations or bids for large purchases;
6. Awards or recommends award of purchase contracts;
7. Tests products for compliance with requirements;
8. Expedites the delivery of purchases;
9. Seeks new products that will perform more advantageously;
10. Participates in the approval of vendors' claims;
11. Supervises handling, storing, and issuing of materials (if a stores operation is maintained);
12. Supervises clerical staff involved in purchasing.

Value analysis. The ultimate test of a purchase resides in its value to the school district. Value is the sum of many factors in the product and in the transaction. It varies from one transaction to the next, even though the vendor, the product, and the price may remain the same. Only the purchasing agent can determine value because it reflects the specific worth of a particular purchase to the school district.

Value is not an abstraction; rather, it is a concrete summation that can, and should, be estimated for each acquisition. Responses to these four questions can help to estimate the value of a product:

1. *Is the quality satisfactory?* The determination of quality standards involves the user as well as the buyer. Usually it is possible to establish a minimum standard of quality for the job to be done. To purchase a product which falls below this standard is foolish, since the performance will be inadequate. To purchase a product which exceeds this standard may be wise, depending on the product's relative price, durability, and additional utility. For example, to purchase fine camel hair brushes for kindergarten children would be an unwarranted excess. But it may be wiser to buy a new book with a library binding—although at slight additional cost—than to buy one with the standard trade binding.

2. *Is the unit being purchased in advantageous quantity?* Small orders frequently have high hidden costs, since the amount of staff effort necessary to complete the purchase is proportionately higher. Larger orders can mean more value when the unit price reflects a quantity dis-

count and the interval before reordering is lengthened. Also to be considered in any quantity decision should be storage space, appropriation limits, and the dangers of deterioration and obsolescence. On this basis it would be wise to order pencils in quantity, since the unit cost would be lower and because pencils are easily stored and do not spoil. But it would be unwise to order mimeograph stencils in great quantity, for although the unit cost would be lower, these products deteriorate in storage.

3. *Is the purchase being sought at the right time?*   In school purchasing, about three quarters of all buying is done in April, May, and June. Frequently, a product can be ordered at lower cost and delivered more expeditiously during a less active period of the year. This is particularly true of transactions involving vendors who deal exclusively with schools.

4. *Will the material be available when needed?*   The product must be available when the user wants it, or it has no value. A biological specimen that arrives a month after completion of study of the related unit is of little worth.

Selection of Goods

Factors in selection.   Selection of supplies and equipment required for the operation of schools should start with the staff member who will ultimately utilize the material purchased. This is a cooperative responsibility which will involve teachers, principals, support personnel, supervisors, and the purchasing agent. Since the program of the schools is constantly changing and since new items are continuously appearing in the market, the selection process is also continuous.

The budget is a controlling element in the selective process. In the case of large units of equipment, most districts require that the requested item be included in the budget. For smaller pieces of equipment and for supply items, the usual practice is to budget a lump sum allowance and to have staff members identify specific needs at a subsequent time. Regardless of the details of budget development, the significant aspect is the dollar allocation, for the amount appropriated in the budget determines both the quantity and the kind of purchases that will be made during the fiscal period.

Standardization.   The goal of standardization is to secure the maximum amount of similarity among items being purchased. Its primary aim is to increase the efficiency of ordering, delivery, storing, and utilizing supplies and equipment. A second aim is to reduce the actual cost that the school district incurs for the materials it purchases.

Standardization does not imply a lowering of quality or a reduction of quantity. It does require analysis of both quality and quantity of an item and could mean alteration in both. A possible result might be the elimination of several different items of the same category in favor of a single unit of higher quality. Standardization concerns itself with such elements as weight, size, finish, composition, grade, and packaging.

There is always a potential hazard that the process of standardization will exceed the bounds of good sense. Overstandardization could stifle the staff effort it seeks to improve. Any program of standardizing should include three traits:

1. Provision for adding or altering standards as needs and products change;
2. Provision to make exceptions where the program warrants more than one kind of an item;
3. An acknowledged point of diminishing returns.

Supply lists. Supply lists are statements describing all the standard or usual supplies that have been identified as needed to conduct the school's program. In some cases the materials on these lists are furnished from a central inventory. More often the lists are used in the development of total district purchase requirements. Total requirements are developed at least annually, although some districts develop their requirements once each quarter or semester.

A supply list can be effective only to the degree that its preparation has been preceded by a study of the standardization of materials. Otherwise, the list runs the risk of containing either too many items or too many omissions. A well-developed supply list reduces the effort required of the teacher or other staff member in identifying and satisfying supply needs.

Each item listed should be described in sufficient detail to enable staff members to distinguish it from other materials. This description should include title, size, color, weight, finish, code number (if used), and unit price. A blank space should be provided in which the number requested may be indicated. Additional blank spaces should be provided for extensions of prices and ordering notations.

Requisitions. A requisition is a written request from the using facility to the purchasing agent for supplies or equipment. In many school districts, the use of requisitions is confined to securing materials that are either not included on a supply list or for which the need was not foreseen at the time the list was prepared.

Identification of the need covered by a requisition most frequently arises with an individual staff member, such as a custodian or teacher. However, the preparation of the written requisition is customarily a responsibility of the building principal or some other person with supervisory responsibility.

By permitting preparation of the written requisition, the supervisor has approved the request. In some cases the requisition is subject to review by the superintendent or his designee. Finally, the accounting function would signify that funds are available for the purchase.

The requisition form contains space to indicate the requested quantity, a complete description, and the price of the item desired. Some districts also provide a space wherein the originator of the requisition may suggest a source of supply. A copy of the requisition is generally retained by the preparing office as a record of the request.

Specifications. Specifications are the written statement of the quality, quantity, and performance the school district requires in a product or group of products. They should define in clear and complete terms the characteristics of the material and the conditions of delivery.

Specifications are always a vital part of any formal purchase contract, as they constitute the basis on which the vendor develops his bid offer. Furthermore, they become the standard for acceptance of the delivered goods. For this reason, they must state unequivocally what is wanted and where it is wanted. In seeking informal quotations, less detailed specifications may be adequate but should be provided.

Specifications can be sound only if they are tailored to the requirements of the particular school district. The writing of specifications is a difficult task because the school orders a wide range of products and few individuals have the technical skill to describe them all well. Wherever standard stock items can be specified, the writing effort is less and the acquisition cost is kept at a minimum. Assistance in developing specifications can also be secured from other school districts, municipalities, some state governments, professional organizations, trade associations, and individual vendors. The General Services Administration of the federal government has an elaborate list of specifications.

Ordering Goods and Services

Normally, ordering will involve only the purchasing staff. In the case of purchase contracts, the board of education is also directly involved since it makes the award. The ordering process is centered about two main factors: purchase orders and bids.

Since close to 75 per cent of orders are now placed in April, May, and June,[2] schools should explore the possibilities of distributing this activity over other months as well in order to take advantage of the potential for lower acquisition costs, more rapid delivery with fewer errors, and a more stabilized work load in the purchasing function.

One current practice is for some school districts of small or medium size to combine into groups for bidding purposes. Thus they concentrate a substantial volume of goods in a single purchase and achieve a maximum quantity discount. In some cases lower costs have resulted. In others, the cost savings have been nominal, if any, and were offset by the effort expended in achieving group decisions on specifications.

Purchase orders. A purchase order is the written instrument that expresses the purchaser's wants to the vendor. The order may be for one or many items. However, very large purchases are usually based on bids. The purchase order is a businesslike method of indicating the school's offer to buy material under clearly stated terms. The order should be issued only after the school district has reasonable assurance that the item is correctly described, available, and properly priced.

A purchase order is a school's offer to buy and is not considered a binding commitment until the vendor accepts it. In theory, the vendor is not bound unless he submits a written acceptance of the

---

[2] "Can School Buying be Done on A Year Round Basis?" *School Management* (February, 1962), 49–53.

purchase order. In practice, many vendors deliver goods without stating their acceptance.

No purchase order should be issued without stipulating an expiration date. Otherwise, the school district might be committed to an unreasonable delay in delivery of a product, but be unable to secure the material elsewhere because an order was outstanding.

After the vendor receives the original of the purchase order, a copy is sent to the agency that requested the material as notification that the goods are on order. A copy is sent to the accounting office to identify an outstanding commitment and to aid in encumbering. The purchasing agent keeps at least one copy for an alphabetical file and a second for a numerical file.

The purchase order form should be printed, with the district identified in the letterhead; and with space for the vendor's name, the quantity, price, description of the product, delivery instructions, coding data, billing instructions, and any additional information which may be required. For control and identification, purchase orders are usually press-numbered. By requiring vendors to list this number on shipments and invoices, the problems of recognition are reduced. The order should be signed by the purchasing agent on behalf of the school district.

Some school districts utilize a combination requisition-purchase order form. The original request is typed on this form and copies are distributed to all related offices. The main advantage of a combination form is the elimination of the clerical effort normally required to type a purchase order. Probably the greatest disadvantage of this method is the likelihood that individual schools, being more remote from contact with vendors, will make errors or omissions in the description or price of the material.

Sometimes it is necessary to amend a purchase order that has been issued and accepted. This can be done with the agreement of the vendor. Some districts utilize a change order form to transcribe the pertinent information. More general practice is to use a standard purchase order form and label it as either amending or replacing the original order.

Bids. A bid is a formal or informal offer by a vendor or contractor to furnish goods or services. Formal bids are sealed, generally requested in compliance with state law, and usually for large purchases. Informal bids are normally requested on smaller purchase transactions and involve oral or written quotations.

Most states require that school districts secure bids on purchases beyond a certain dollar amount. The purpose of such legislation is generally twofold:

1. To insure that purchasing is conducted on an objective and competitive basis;
2. To guarantee the purchase of material at the lowest possible price.

A survey published by the Association of School Business Officials of the United States and Canada [3] indicated that thirty-three states have laws requiring the bidding of supply purchases. The total amount of the purchase determines whether or not a school district is requried to take bids on the transaction. Some states vary the requirement for different school districts, permitting larger districts to expend higher amounts without bidding. The amount of supply purchases exempt from the bid law requirement varied from $100 in Tennessee to $6000 in Ohio city school districts.

Most school officials agree that bidding generally results in a dollar savings for the school district. The additional effort required to develop formal bids is usually offset by the lower offers received. This is true in the aggregate, despite cases where items cost more under bid procedures than by open-market purchase. Existing bid laws can be improved by remedying three weaknesses:

1. Frequently the legal maximum which may be expended without bids is unrealistically low. This means a school district is constantly asking for bids on all sorts of materials. The cost of preparing specifications, advertising and distributing them, and opening and analyzing bids for small purchases exceeds the dollar savings in price. Furthermore, the delay can inhibit the program.
2. Bidding puts a premium on price at the sacrifice of quality. Bid laws emphasize lowest price, and may encourage a vendor to offer goods of marginal quality. If the product is later found wanting, the district has difficulty in rejecting delivery. More important, the program is impeded because material of proper quality is not available.
3. The focus on lowest bid price has forced some vendors to reduce their staffs in order to remain competitive. The amount of service and

---

[3] David McCurrach, "N.S.S.E.A. Summary of Minimum Bid Laws by States," *School Business Affairs,* Vol. 28, No. 4 (April, 1962), 18.

attention a school district can expect is thus greatly reduced. In some cases this extra care and concern are worth more to the school's operation than the several dollars saved in bidding.

In some cases the legal requirement is satisfied by informal bidding. In others, specifications must be prepared and advertised, sealed bids must be opened, and an award must be made by the board of education. State laws specify that the award of the bid shall be made to the lowest responsible bidder who meets the specifications and the terms of the bid opening. Rejection of bidders as not responsible has probably caused more legal actions than any other element in vendor-school district relations. Unless there exists evidence of arbitrary or capricious judgment, the courts have almost universally sustained the determinations of vendor responsibility made by boards of education.

Determining responsibility or lack of it is a difficult task. The vendor would not be in business unless he had been able to sell to some buyers. But the school administration and the board of education have an obligation to accept only that low bidder who can perform satisfactorily. The best evidence is a vendor's past record with the school district. In the absence of this an opinion can be formed best on the basis of:

1. An inspection of his premises and his records;
2. An investigation of his performance with other buyers, preferably school districts.

Supply Management

Supply management is the culmination of the purchasing effort: the handling of supplies from their arrival from the vendor until their distribution for consumption. It involves delivery, storage, and distribution. Sound procedures are indispensable in supply management because of the high cost of supply materials in the volume handled by school districts and because the worth of a supply is measured by its being available where and when needed.

Delivery. Delivery or receiving of supplies involves checking the shipment and assigning the material. Checking a shipment starts with an examination of the shipping ticket or bill of lading by a school employee designated to accept shipments. Since most trucking firms will want a signed delivery ticket, the first step is to verify that the number of parcels delivered equals the number listed. The parcels are subsequently opened and an item count is made. This is verified against the shipping ticket and the original purchase order. Once checked in, materials are moved from the delivery area to be stored or used.

The receiving area for light packages can be an office. However, the delivery area for heavier shipments must have a heavy duty floor, be well-lighted, and be accessible to delivery vehicles. In individual schools this area should be located adjacent to the custodian's storage area.

Some large school districts prefer a centralized system of receiving: all supplies are delivered to a single receiving point and later redistributed. Usually, these districts also provide centralized storage. Those favoring this method argue that shipping costs are lower if only one delivery point is specified and supplies and records are more efficiently handled if received by skilled workers in a well-equipped location.

In decentralized shipments, orders are delivered directly to each school and stored there. Those favoring this plan feel it saves the double handling and reshipment required under centralized receiving.

Storage. A school must maintain an adequate inventory of consumable materials or its operations will be chaotic. The amount of inventory should be related to purchasing, since the volume should be sufficient to generate a maximum quantity discount. Further, the stock on hand should not be less than will be consumed before a reorder can be delivered. Inventory volume should not exceed shelf life, nor should inventories be maintained beyond the capacity to provide proper storage.

Most schools plan to open the school year with a full year's instructional supplies on hand. An exception is made for certain seasonal or perishable materials, which are provided on an as-needed basis. Large school districts with well-organized purchasing and supply management functions frequently maintain smaller inventories with more frequent replenishment.

Inventory can be either centralized or stored in individual school buildings. Centralized warehousing is most apt to have merit in the larger districts. Advantages claimed include more efficient use of staff and reduction of the efforts of school building personnel. Centralized warehousing can mean better inventory control, superior storage methods, and a wider variety of materials. Improvements in inventory control include elimination of hoarding, reduction of pilferage, and adherence to first in-first out consumption. Another advantage is that shipping costs are reduced by eliminating drop shipments. For central warehousing to operate efficiently, an adequate staff and functional warehouse space must be provided.

Decentralized storage within the individual school is usually the soundest practice in small and medium-sized school districts. Those favoring this method cite as advantages lower total costs, less red tape in securing supplies, and availability of the supplies as needed and where needed.

Distribution. The final action in supply management is distribution of inventoried materials to the staff member who will consume these in his work. An effective distribution plan is simple in structure, prompt in response, and accurate in its deliveries. Distribution must include a record of what is wanted and a control on what has been provided and where it went.

The simplest method of distribution occurs when the school building is provided with all of the supplies requested in the annual requisition. The school office may then utilize individual staff member requisitions to distribute the gross order to final destinations. Of course, some materials will be stored in a common area within the school building. Staff members then draw upon these supplies as needed and, usually, unimpeded.

Some schools requisition total annual requirements but store these in the building in a common pool. When a staff member wishes to replenish his supply, he originates a stockroom requisition form which is filled from the building's inventory.

If the school system has a central warehouse, the distribution of inventoried material is usually made in response to a storeroom requisition. This is approved by the principal and forwarded to the business office, where the cost of the material is charged against the school's budgetary appropriation. The warehouse then fills the order, usually delivering the material to the building by a district-operated vehicle traversing a regular circuit route covering all school buildings.

Ethics of Purchasing

The buyer-seller relationship has always been fraught with hazards for both parties. Tremendous sums of money hinge on school district decisions to purchase one product rather than another. In such circumstances, both the purchasing agent and the salesman are under considerable pressure. This condition can readily deteriorate into dishonest practice unless the purchasing agent exercises extreme care in his vendor relationships.

True, both the purchasing agent and the sales representative have an obligation to conduct themselves ethically. But the school district must have primary concern for the proper behavior of its agent. Because the school district purchasing agent is working with the public's money, it is doubtful that any standard of deportment can be too scrupulous.

High standards of personal conduct exist only when the individual purchasing agent possesses strength of character. These traits cannot be legislated or acquired on the job, but must be sought for in applicants for the position. Beyond care in the selection of the purchasing officer, the best guarantee that purchasing practices are sound is an established routine that diffuses elements of purchasing under the total coordination of the purchasing agent.

The purchasing agent with integrity recognizes his duty toward his employer, his position, and himself. The school district has the reciprocal obligation of acknowledging his responsible position by providing him with adequate staff and facilities, just compensation, and worthy recognition.

Many professional organizations have recognized the importance of developing a general statement of ethical behavior that the individual school administrator can utilize as a guide. The general statement or code is not a substitute for sound individual judgment; rather, it seeks to guide the individual in developing these judgments. One of the best codes of ethics is that adopted in 1954 by the New York State Association of School Business Officials.

Code of Ethics for School Purchasing Officials

1. To consider first the interests of the school district and the betterment of its educational program.

2. To endeavor to obtain the greatest value for every tax dollar expended.

3. To be receptive to advice and suggestions from colleagues, both in the educational field and in other departments of business administration, insofar as such advice and suggestions are not in conflict with legal or moral restrictions in purchasing procedures.

4. To strive for knowledge of school equipment and supplies in order to recommend items that may either reduce cost or increase the efficiency of the means of education.

5. To insist on and expect honesty in sales representation whether offered verbally or in writing, through the medium of advertising or in the sample of a product submitted.

6. To give all responsible bidders equal consideration and the assurance of unbiased judgment in determining whether their product meets specifications and the educational needs of the district.

7. To discourage the offer of, and to decline, gifts which in any way might influence the purchase of school equipment and supplies.

8. To accord a prompt and courteous reception, insofar as conditions permit, to all who call on legitimate business missions.

9. To counsel and assist fellow school purchasing officials in the performance of their duties whenever occasion permits.

10. To cooperate with educational governmental and trade associations in the promotion and development of sound business methods in the procurement of school equipment and supplies.

CHAPTER V

Insurance

Fundamentals

Insurance may be defined as the transfer of financial risk from one principal to another principal or group better able to assume it. There are three major categories of insurance protection for school districts:

1. *Property protection* against financial loss arising from damage to owned property;
2. *Liability protection* against loss arising from unintentional property damage or personal injury for which the school is liable;
3. *Crime protection* against loss arising from illegal acts, such as embezzlement or theft.

A fourth category of protection being sought by an increasing number of schools is personal welfare coverage. This is designed to protect employees and students against hazards to their physical well-being.

Legal requirements. The legal authority of boards of education to purchase insurance protection is widely recognized, either explicitly or implicitly. In some instances state law or regulation may require the local district to have specific protection. In some states the law or regulation is merely permissive. Where neither explicit law nor regulation exist, the courts have frequently held that boards of education have the implied authority to provide insurance protection.

Insurance and safety. One cannot consider insurance protection without relating it to safety, for insurance transfers or spreads the risk, but safety tends to contain or diminish the risk. The more effective the safety program, the less risk there is to be transferred. Thus, from the standpoint of both economic and human values, the safety program is a vital concomitant of insurance protection.

Insurance carriers recognize the importance of safety in reduction of claims and expense and are active in promoting safety among their clients. They inspect the insured's premises, make recommendations designed to reduce hazards, and publicize programs of safety education.

Sources of insurance.   Most insurance is purchased from private firms, the majority of which are either stock or mutual organizations. A stock insurance company has sold stock, elected a board of directors, and engaged in the insurance business with the goal of returning a profit on the investment made by the stockholders. Stock insurance companies vary in size and quality, in services offered, in types of risk insured, and—despite common belief—in rates charged for protection.

Mutual companies are incorporated organizations that do not issue stock. A board of directors is elected from among the policyholders. The charge for insurance is usually collected by advance premiums, as is done by stock companies. Mutual firms typically plan to return a portion of this premium as a dividend on the expiration of the policy. Some mutuals still issue policies with an assessment clause, permitting them to levy an additional charge if the losses experienced are in excess of the premiums charged. Mutual companies, too, vary in scope, quality, and rate structure.

Occasionally, insurance is purchased from an assessment or reciprocal organization. An assessment company requires its members to make a deposit at the time of initial coverage. Thereafter the policyholder is given a periodic assessment to cover the loss experience. A reciprocal organization is a group of persons or firms, each carrying insurance with the organization. In case of loss, each subscriber is liable for a pro rata share of the cost.

State insurance plans.   These are programs operated by the state government for the protection of public property, including local school districts. According to Viles,[1] five states (Alabama, North Carolina, North Dakota, South Carolina, and Wisconsin) have state-operated insurance programs covering public schools. These plans are generally fully supported by the premiums paid by local school districts. Usually the state plans distribute a portion of the risks to commercial insurance firms by purchasing reinsurance.

---

[1] N. E. Viles, Sr., *School Property Insurance Experiences at State Level,* U.S. Office of Education Bulletin 1956, No. 7 (Washington, D.C.: USGPO, 1956).

Self-insurance. To self-insure, the district accepts all, or most of the insurable risk, and foregoes the usual insurance coverage. All districts accept self-insurance for small exposures, such as the disappearance of a library book, a jar of paste, or a basketball. But self-insurance for large property loss or liability risks is prudent only in very large school districts.

Purchasing insurance. Commercial insurance is usually purchased from an agent or a broker. An agent is a representative of the insurance company, normally having the authority to bind the company for the insurance risks facing public schools. A broker is usually considered a representative of the purchaser and does not have this authority.

State laws sometimes modify the agent-broker distinction. An understanding of this difference is essential, particularly when coverage is initiated and when premiums are being paid. Many firms which provide insurance to school districts engage in direct writing of policies—that is, purchasing services are provided directly by an employee of the insurance company. Where state plans exist, the policies are usually issued on a direct-writing basis.

Fire Insurance

There are approximately 4000 school fires in the United States each year. Fortunately most of these fires result in only minor losses. However, the potential of extreme loss is always present and fire insurance is the most common type of insurance protection carried by school districts.

Coverages and endorsements. The basic fire insurance policy covers a building, with or without its contents, against loss arising from fire or lightning or from damage by water or chemicals used to extinguish the fire.

Because many potential perils were not protected by this basic coverage, insurance companies now provide policy endorsements, whereby the property is covered for a variety of related hazards. The two most common endorsements issued with fire insurance are:

1. *Extended coverage.* This provides protection against the hazards of windstorm, hail, explosion, riot, civil commotion, accidents of aircraft or vehicles, and smoke damage.

2. *Vandalism and malicious mischief.* This protects the school district against property damage caused by cranks, trespassers, or pranksters.

Other endorsements are frequently available, including glass breakage, unexpired premiums, fallen buildings, explosion, and extra expense protection. However, school districts generally confine their additional protection to the Extended Coverage and Vandalism and Malicious Mischief endorsements.

Rates. Development of fire insurance rates is a complicated task, generally performed for insurance companies by rate-making organizations. Small exposures, such as homes, are covered by an average rate for the type of property. Large exposures, such as schools, are normally assigned an individual rate, based on an engineer's study of the particular structure and its environment.

The total fire insurance rate includes consideration of several factors:

1. Location of the property;
2. Kind and amount of fire protection available;
3. Kind of construction;
4. Kinds of endorsements added to basic protection;
5. Length of the policy term;
6. Proportion of actual value covered by insurance.

Many school officials believe that public schools pay fire insurance rates that are disproportionately high in relation to actual school fire losses. This position is supported by several surveys sponsored by the Association of School Business Officials. Results of the most recent survey [2] indicated that school districts received in loss settlements only 31.8 per cent of the total premiums paid during the period 1946–55. In contrast, in 1954 the average loss ratio for all fire insurance companies was 57.2 per cent.

Part of this rate problem arises because all educational institutions, public and private, are grouped as one for fire insurance rate development. Many believe that public schools are built and operated under higher standards of fire safety than are privately owned

---

[2] Paul B. Salmon, *Fire Insurance Principles and Practices,* Association of School Business Officials of the United States and Canada, Bulletin No. 18 (Evanston, Ill.: The Association, 1958).

properties. If public schools could be separately rated, which thus far has not been done, experience and rates might be lower.

Co-insurance. Fire insurance policies for large risks, such as school districts, are frequently written with a co-insurance clause. This clause obligates the school district to maintain insurance at a certain percentage, generally 80 per cent (but sometimes higher) of the actual cash value of the property. In return for this guarantee that fire policy amounts will be maintained at a high percentage of actual value, the insurance company offers substantial reductions in rates.

As the title indicates, this is a *co*-insurance arrangement, involving both the insured and insurer in a loss. If a loss occurs and the school district has maintained the proper amounts of insurance (such as 80 per cent of actual value), the company will pay all of the claim up to the declared value of the policy. However, if the school district fails to maintain insurance amounts at the stipulated percentage of actual value, it may be penalized in proportion to its underinsurance. Thus, co-insurance has an advantage in cost that can be exploited only if care is taken to establish and maintain accurate declared values.

Insurance appraisals. The fire insurance policy is designed to protect values; it is therefore imperative that current sound insurable values of the building and its contents be known. An appraisal is an orderly procedure designed to establish and maintain correct valuations for structures and contents. In turn, the insurance policy must reflect these accurate figures. With such a program, the school district can avoid wasteful overinsurance, or a possible co-insurance penalty if underinsured, and will have the documentation needed to prove values at the time of loss.

The ideal appraisal is that furnished by a commercial appraisal company. These firms specialize in this activity and provide competent, independent appraisals. Some school districts secure an appraisal from the insurance company. Although such an appraisal is free, it is usually a rough approximation of value rather than a precise and detailed estimate. Other districts use their own staff members to compute appraised values. Such a procedure can be valid for the appraisal of contents but is frequently less accurate in the appraisal of building values. Finally, some schools use engineers or contractors to prepare appraisals, a procedure which can be adequate if the surveyor is competent.

Public and institutional property plan. A recent development in most states has been the appearance of public and institutional plan insurance. This affords combined protection against fire loss and related perils, usually at a substantial savings over regular rates for these coverages. As the name implies, this plan is offered to schools, churches, hospitals and similar institutions. The plan can eliminate the hazard of a co-insurance penalty, since the policy values are written on an "agreed amount," accepted by both insurer and insured.

Liability Insurance

Liability insurance protects the school district against financial loss arising from liability for personal injury or property damage. Public school districts are not subject to liability action unless state laws permit it. Only five states have specifically removed this general immunity from liability actions, but these include the two largest: California and New York. Furthermore, a recent study[3] revealed that at least fifteen states permit school districts to secure liability insurance, even though the district might otherwise claim immunity. Where the district does carry such liability insurance, the law sometimes prohibits the insurance carrier from using immunity as a defense.

"Save harmless" laws, which are part of the state laws in New Jersey, New York, and Connecticut, place the school district in a situation where liability protection is essential. These laws stipulate that the school district will save staff members from financial loss for any liability claim against them arising out of their scope of employment. Thus, the law imposes a distinct and direct liability on the school district.

If the school district is obligated or elects to carry this protection, it finds it advantageous to secure all its liability insurance from one company. This prevents possible conflict between two different carriers over an occurrence that might be covered under two different

---

[3] National Education Association, National Commission on Safety Education, *Who Is Liable For Pupil Injuries?* (Washington, D.C.: The Association, 1963).

policies. For example, an injury to a pupil while boarding a school bus on school premises could involve the general liability carrier or the automobile liability carrier. Furthermore, combining liability policies frequently results in a discount on total premium charges.

General liability insurance. This is designed to provide broad coverage against liability actions involving the school or its employees, and may be issued on a scheduled or comprehensive basis. The trend is toward comprehensive policies, because the insured is protected for both known and unknown hazards. With a scheduled policy, the school district is protected only for the exposures listed on the schedule.

General liability usually includes hazards arising out of ownership or operation of school facilities. It should include products liability if the school operates a cafeteria. Frequently it will include protection against negligence on the part of school employees in the performance of their duties. Liability for automobile operations is ordinarily covered under a separate policy, although in some states it is available in a comprehensive liability policy.

Automobile liability insurance. This protects the school district for personal injuries to others or damage to their property arising from the operation of the school district's automobiles, buses, and trucks. Most states now either require or permit this coverage for district-owned school bus operations. School districts that contract for such private service may also need to safeguard the district's interests by including hired automobiles in their liability policy.

Another provision of the automobile liability policy covers non-ownership liability. This protects the school district against loss resulting from accidents involving vehicles owned by staff members and operated in connection with school business.

Boiler and machinery insurance. This affords protection against loss or damage due to the explosion or rupture of a boiler or its parts caused by steam or water pressure. The district may insure its properties against the hazard of explosions under a fire policy endorsement, but such coverage excludes steam boilers. Typically, boiler insurance covers damage to the boiler and to other school property, and damage to property owned by others. It may also include bodily injury liability protection.

This policy may be broadened to cover a sudden and accidental cracking of a cast metal boiler and the bulging of a boiler due to steam, water, or the lack of steam or water. One of the most valuable features of boiler insurance is the provision that the insurance carrier will provide regular inspection of the boiler plant. Insurance companies that specialize in boiler insurance maintain skilled inspectors who regularly examine boilers and other pressure vessels for the insured. This inspection service, designed to prevent defective conditions that might lead to explosions, frequently justifies the expenditure for the insurance coverage.

Workmen's compensation insurance. Usually, school districts are liable for compensating employees who are injured while performing their jobs. In some cases, recovery is a liability action; in others, workmen's compensation laws stipulate the amount and kind of benefits to be paid. These laws provide weekly benefits equal to no more than two thirds of the lost income. Medical payments usually cover the cost of treatment. Partial or total disability is compensated by either a flat sum or extended payments. Death benefits vary according to earnings and number of dependents.

Other Insurance

Fidelity bonds. Fidelity bonds protect the school district against loss arising from fraudulent or dishonest actions by its officers and employees. Whereas insurance is a contract between the carrier and the school district, a bond is really a three-party contract. The company guarantees to protect the school district against financial loss arising from the actions of an employee.

In theory, the company suffers no loss, since it is guaranteeing that the employee will perform the actions required by the bond. If the company felt that a particular employee would not merit this guarantee, it would refuse to bond him.

Fidelity bonds are usually issued in three different classifications:

1. *Statutory public officials bonds* guarantee the faithful performance of duties as well as the honesty of public officials. The requirement for these bonds, as well as the nature and extent of the protection afforded, is specified in the statute. These bonds are written on an individual basis.

2. *Schedule bonds* protect against loss arising from the actions of one or more members of a list of employees. The schedule can be based on either a list of names or a list of positions. A list of positions is usually more desirable because it eliminates the need to notify the company when personnel are replaced.

3. *Blanket bonds* guarantee the honest actions of all staff members. The number of positions to be covered is established at the start of the year and the company's premium is based on this figure. However, if changes in the number of persons employed occur during the year, they are covered automatically and without extra charge.

Contract bonds. A contract bond is a surety bond involving an outside individual or firm and the school district. The bond guarantees that the named individual or firm will perform a transaction in compliance with specified conditions. In some cases, these bonds are required by good business practice; in others, specific statutes compel their use.

There are three types of contract bonds:

1. *Bid bonds* are guarantees that the company submitting a bid will, if awarded the contract, enter into the contract and file performance and payment bonds.

2. *Performance bonds* offer the surety company's guarantee that the firm awarded a contract will faithfully perform the contract. Most school districts require these for all construction contracts and large service or supply contracts.

3. *Payment bonds* guarantee that the contractor has paid for all labor and material utilized in the contract with the school. This protects the school district against nonpayment claims of suppliers and subcontractors, which are permissible in some states.

Automobile physical damage insurance. Automobile physical damage insurance protects against the loss or damage of automotive equipment. The two major types of coverage are for collision or upset and comprehensive loss or damage. Collision or upset insurance covers damage to the school's vehicle caused by impact with another object, moving or stationary. Comprehensive coverage indemnifies for almost all other perils, including fire, theft, explosion, glass breakage, vandalism, hail, water, riot, falling objects, and windstorms.

Many schools operating fleets of vehicles do not secure collision or upset insurance because of the high cost in relation to their exposure. Where collision insurance is obtained it is usually obtained with a $100 or greater deductible amount, thereby reducing the premium. Comprehensive loss coverage is relatively low in cost and is frequently considered a sound investment.

Burglary, robbery, and theft insurance. Because schools handle large sums of money and contain valuable supplies and equipment, they need protection against loss arising from the crimes of others. Burglary is defined as the felonious entry into the premises by force or violence. Robbery is the felonious taking of money or other property by the use or threat of violence. Theft is the stealing or taking of money or property of another.

There are four principal forms of insurance coverage for these contingencies:

1. *Safe burglary* protects against the loss of money and property from within a locked safe or vault, provided there is evidence of forced entry.

2. *Mercantile open stock* covers loss of supplies, equipment, fixtures and merchandise, but excludes cash and securities. The loss must occur while the premises are closed and there must be evidence of forced entry.

3. *Inside and outside robbery* safeguards against loss of cash, securities, or property by robbery. (Sometimes the two coverages are written as separate policies.)

4. *Broad form, money, and securities* affords the widest protection against loss of money and securities. It covers the destruction, disappearance, or wrongful abstraction of cash and securities, as well as property damage or loss caused by safe burglary or robbery.

Property floater. A property floater policy is an all-risk coverage of specific articles while on or off the premises. The protected items are listed in a schedule and are assigned values. The policy usually covers all potential forms of loss, except such obvious exceptions as wear and tear, action of vermin, and willful destruction. Schools find this coverage advantageous in protecting expensive objects, such as motion picture projectors, typewriters, and musical instruments.

Personal welfare insurance. A category of insurance sought by an increasing number of school districts provides personal welfare coverage. This is designed to protect staff members, their dependents, and—occasionally—pupils. Protection may be afforded under life, accident, hospitalization, surgical, health, and disability insurance policies. Costs may be borne by either the school district or the employee, or may be shared by both.

CHAPTER VI

Operation and Maintenance

The Program and Its Coordination

Need. The present value of public school buildings and the equipment housed in these structures is between thirty-five and forty billion dollars. Each year, about three billion dollars are expended for new construction and equipment.

A well-constructed school building has a reasonable useful life of at least fifty years. The school's physical life—that is, the time-span during which the structure can effectively shelter its occupants —is probably twice that long. The functional life of the original facility, the period in which the structure serves as an adequate environment for an instructional program, the nature of which changes over the years, may well be less than fifty years. By proper concern for maintaining, altering, and improving the physical plant, this functional life may be greatly increased.

Definitions. Operation of plant consists of those activities concerned with opening the school plant and keeping it in a safe and comfortable condition during use. It involves cleaning, heating, and lighting the school building, as well as maintaining plant security. The school custodians are the personnel who discharge most of these operational responsibilities.

Maintenance of plant involves those elements related to preserving, repairing, and protecting the school plant, its equipment, and the school grounds. It is not concerned with day-to-day tasks, but with a longer cycle. Although the maintenance mechanic is the school employee who personifies the maintenance program, some of the maintenance work may be performed by outside contractors.

School districts usually allocate 12–15 per cent of annual current budgets to these two functions. The types of buildings and their ages, the kind of educational program, local standards of cleanliness, climatic conditions, levels of service and maintenance, and the area wage structure all contribute to this variance. Usual experience is that approximately two thirds of this expenditure will be for operation of plant and the remaining one third for maintenance.

In the day-to-day operation of a school, it is sometimes quite difficult to distinguish between where operation of plant effort ends and where maintenance of plant activity begins. Chances are that this lack of distinction is a sign of a good organization. The school custodian, who is principally responsible for plant operation, is assigned some maintenance responsibilities. Thus, as he goes about his daily routine, he will be giving regular attention to certain preventive or periodic maintenance work.

The administrative direction of plant operation and maintenance is the responsibility of the superintendent of schools. However, in most school districts, operation and maintenance are delegated by the superintendent to a subordinate administrator.

Usually a position of assistant superintendent of schools for plant management exists only in the largest school districts. Medium-sized districts frequently assign this responsibility to a superintendent of buildings and grounds who reports to the school business administrator. In smaller districts with smaller staffs, the business administrator or the superintendent of schools has a direct responsibility for managing the buildings and grounds program. Where unit control is not in effect, the superintendent of buildings and grounds may report directly to the board of education.

Superintendent of buildings and grounds

Qualifications. It is difficult to identify a single set of qualifications as absolute prerequisites to successful performance. It is, however, reasonable to outline the main characteristics that the newcomer seeking to establish a professional career should possess.

The professional superintendent of buildings and grounds should be a college graduate with a major in architecture, engineering, or a related field and he should have had several years of practical experience in building construction, operation, and maintenance. Some of this experience should have been gained in a position involving managerial responsibility.

There is presently a dearth of individuals with this combination of training and experience. Indeed, many boards of education are not willing or able to offer salaries that will attract this level of professional skill. As a result, the practicalities of the situation demand that educational qualifications must, in many cases, be compromised.

Responsibilities. The nature and degree of responsibility assigned to a superintendent of buildings and grounds should be related to the abilities of the incumbent and the size, complexity, and staff of the school district. The most common responsibilities include:

1. Preparation of budget estimates for operations and maintenance;
2. Overseeing of expenditures of operation and maintenance appropriations;
3. Development of contract specifications and supervision of contractors;
4. Maintenance of consumption, repair, and cost records;
5. Development of long-range maintenance plans;
6. Recruitment, training, assignment, and supervision of personnel.

Staffing the Custodial Force

Number and qualifications. The number of custodians required to staff a school depends largely on local standards of housekeeping. A school with a high standard will undoubtedly require more manpower than a school of similar size that is less discriminating.

A number of manpower formulas have been developed to establish approximate custodial staff requirements for specific work loads. Perhaps the most refined technique for determining manpower needs is that developed by Linn.[1] He has described all the individual custodial tasks that might be assigned and has established a time value in minutes for each. The sum of the time value multiplied by the frequency with which each task is performed gives a total work load in minutes. This total is divided by the number of minutes in the custodian's work day and the result is the manpower required.

There is, of course, no single set of qualifications that all able custodians meet. This does not mean that there are no particular

---

[1] H. H. Linn, L. C. Helm, and K. P. Grabarkiewicz, *School Custodian's Housekeeping Handbook* (New York: Teachers College, Bureau of Publications, Columbia University, 1948), pp. 46–54.

qualifications for the position. Rather, it indicates that there should be some flexibility in their development and interpretation.

Six key standards in selecting custodians are:

1. Neat appearance;
2. Excellent physical condition;
3. Pleasant personality and excellent character;
4. Mental alertness;
5. Above-average mechanical aptitude;
6. Loyalty to fellow staff members.

Relationships and assignment.   The principal of a school building usually has complete authority and responsibility for the conduct of staff and program in his particular school. From this concept flows the thought that the school custodian should have a responsibility to, and receive guidance and direction from, the building principal. In this manner the operating personnel will make a maximum contribution to the school's educational program.

The superintendent of buildings and grounds also has authority over the custodian. Chances are that he hired him and gave him his indoctrination. In addition, he furnishes many of the products and tools the custodian uses and is largely responsible for his present and future assignments.

The existence of two superiors should not make for conflict since they will normally share this authority and exercise it with mutual respect. The building principal is more apt to be interested in coordinating the custodian's role with the instructional program of the school. The superintendent of buildings and grounds is normally concerned with technical aspects of performance: time schedules, proper selection and use of materials, correct work methods, and standards of cleanliness.

Assignment of custodians to particular schools is usually the responsibility of the superintendent of buildings and grounds. In making these assignments, he will evaluate the skill and personality of the custodian in relation to the needs of a specific building and its staff.

The superintendent of buildings and grounds maintains close liaison with the custodian and with the building principal. He furnishes technical advice when such a question arises and he counsels with both principal and custodian in cases of minor conflict. But the superintendent of buildings and grounds must oversee the operation of many buildings while the building principal has total responsibility for but one. Being in the building at all times, the principal can make needed on-the-spot decisions. He can serve to coordinate teaching staff requests that might otherwise overwhelm the custodian.

Training. Rarely does a new custodial staff member have previous experience in public school operations. Therefore, the training that the new custodian receives after he is hired is most significant in establishing his effectiveness as a worker. As the complexity of school buildings has increased, school administrators have recognized the necessity of systematic training for all custodial personnel.

The responsibility for organizing, supervising, and evaluating a training program is typically delegated to the superintendent of buildings and grounds. Size, location, and sophistication of the district will determine the methods employed in training. Common to almost all beginning training is the use of the "buddy system," under which a new custodian is assigned to a competent experienced custodian to learn the day-to-day routines and techniques. The "buddy system" is frequently combined with other more formal training.

Sound custodial training will involve all custodians and will be continuous, as there are always new products to be explored and there is always the need to review and remind.

Work schedules. The bulk of custodial effort is predictable, routine, and measurable. A work schedule establishes what tasks a custodian in a particular building is responsible for, when he should perform them, and how long each should take. It is essential to have such an assignment to insure orderly discharge of the custodian's duties.

A work schedule should be cooperatively developed, involving the custodian as well as the building principal and the superintendent of buildings and grounds. It should be realistic in what must be done and in the time allotted to each task. The schedule should be flexible, since it cannot always be followed precisely. Time should be allowed for minor repairs, odd jobs, and services to teachers and other staff members.

With a forty-hour work week as the usual standard, most schools find that a single day-shift of custodians cannot adequately clean and service the building. A large number of schools employ a group of custodians who work a late afternoon and evening-shift and complete the major share of the cleaning program.

Inspection and supervision. Regular inspection is an integral element in developing and maintaining acceptable housekeeping standards. Formal inspections should be made by the principal and the superintendent of buildings and grounds, preferably together, on a periodic basis. The real value of inspection resides in its ability to improve standards. Therefore it is essential that any deficiencies observed be brought to the attention of the custodian as promptly as possible.

The daily observations by the principal and the superintendent of buildings and grounds constitute informal inspections. These can reveal unsatisfactory conditions before they develop into major problems.

Custodial supplies and equipment. If the custodian is to perform effectively, he must have a wide range of supplies and equipment. Proper supplies and equipment lead to better utilization of the custodian's time and energies.

It is estimated that 90–95 per cent of the expense of the average custodial job in a school is for the labor involved and only 5–10 per cent is spent for supplies. The cost of tools and equipment is difficult to compute on a job basis, but the long period of utility for most tools renders these costs relatively low.

Selection. The initial step in the acquisition of supplies and equipment is the identification of needs and the selection of products. Major responsibility for coordinating this process is usually assigned to the superintendent of buildings and grounds or the business administrator. The effort should involve the individual custodians, who are the ultimate users of the products selected.

Many school districts focus the selection process on a standardized list of custodial materials. Considerable effort is required to establish an initial list but, once developed, the standardized list will save much time. The list can be used over several years with minor changes, and should simplify requisitioning, ordering, and inventory procedures.

Procurement. Procurement of custodial materials, like all purchasing, should be the responsibility of the school district's business office. These purchases should be made on the basis of standards and specifications established under the leadership of the superintendent of buildings and grounds. The decision to accept or reject a product should be a cooperative one, involving the business office and the superintendent of buildings and grounds.

Storage. It is usual for schools to make certain custodial supply purchases once or twice annually and to rely on their inventory for intervening periods. Some caution must be exercised in the storing of materials with a short shelf life.

Supplies can be stored in a central warehouse, in the individual schools, or in both. For the storage of custodial materials in the school building, a dry, secure, and accessible location with a fairly even temperature is required. Records should be kept of both stock on hand and consumption rate. Stock should be consumed on the basis of first in-first out.

Maintenance of Plant

Need for long-range plan. Most of the projects involved in the normal maintenance of the plant can be foreseen and should be included in a program that covers a period of five or ten years. Such a plan will help to stabilize annual budget appropriations for maintenance. Also, long-range planning will help minimize failures which might arise from the lack of an adequate program of maintenance. To be effective, the planning should be continuous and brought up to date before each annual budget is drawn up.

Among considerations to be included in developing a long-range maintenance plan are heating, plumbing, ventilation, painting, electrical systems, roofing, and structural and grounds needs. The sole significant exception to long-range planning will be emergency maintenance. Most frequently, this results from storm damage or from an unforeseen failure of part of the structure or its equipment. To a degree, the extent of emergency failures is reduced by an adequate long-range program.

Preventive maintenance. Preventive maintenance includes work of a relatively minor nature, designed to insure trouble-free operation of the building and its equipment and performed without prior observation of a defect. Examples of preventive maintenance are the cleaning and replacing of air filters, the replacing of ropes and chains, the lubrication of motors and bearings, and some painting. Ordinarily the need for any of these tasks is not obvious before the work is performed; rather the work is done to prevent later failure.

Recurring and periodic maintenance. Recurring maintenance consists of jobs that are undertaken at least once a year. These include the servicing of the entire heating plant before the onset of the heating season. Certain types of floor maintenance are considered recurring tasks, as is the care of pupil desks and chairs. Lawn, shrub, and tree maintenance is largely a recurring task, particularly the feeding and pruning operations.

Periodic maintenance includes those jobs that are done only once every several years. Painting is the most common periodic maintenance task and the need for this varies between three years and eight years, depending on surface, exposure, and standards. Plumbing and heating system components are involved in periodic maintenance, as are window shades, venetian blinds and draperies, weatherstripping, caulking, exterior masonry, and roof decks. Furniture and apparatus also require periodic repairs.

Deferred maintenance. Whenever the competition for funds in a public school budget becomes severe, the maintenance program faces a real hazard. In such circumstances, some school districts defer maintenance projects until later budget periods. The practice of deferring maintenance is perilous because such a delay may compromise the safety of the staff and student body and lead to ultimately greater expenditures.

The safest way to approach plant maintenance expenditures is to accept the concept of an annual expenditure of about 2 per cent of the initial cost of construction to protect the original investment and utility. This percentage is almost a fixed charge over the period of occupancy of the structure. There is some opportunity to exercise prudence in scheduling or delaying certain projects. But the bulk of maintenance costs are determined by the nature and use of school buildings.

Records. The extensive nature of some repairs, the significant costs of certain maintenance work, and the need to recall previous activity all point to the necessity of accurate record keeping. Maintenance records usually contain three kinds of data: inventory, cost, and condition.

Inventory records have greatest value in a district that supports a maintenance parts, supplies, and equipment inventory. In such cases a record should be kept of the quality, type, and disposition of these items. For parts and supplies, such a record reveals patterns of use and serves as a guide in reordering and control. For equipment, it assists in establishing accountability for valuable school district property.

Cost records assist in charging maintenance expenditures to budgetary appropriations. They serve as valuable aids in preparing estimates for future budgets. Cost records can be used to compare expenses for a particular job performed by district personnel with the fee charged by outside contractors. These records are also valuable for making cost comparisons between two or more different materials used for a similar kind of maintenance work.

Condition records indicate the nature and timing of recurring maintenance actions, such as the replacement of an air filter or the lubrication of an electric motor. These records should be kept by the person responsible for the particular maintenance action and should indicate the date on which the work was last done. Such data can be shown on a large chart, and time cycles for various jobs may be included to help develop future maintenance schedules.

District Personnel Versus Outside Contractors

A school district may accomplish its maintenance work either by staffing and equipping its own force or by engaging outside contractors. Long debate has been held over the relative advantages of one plan over the other.

Those who favor using school employees for maintenance work assert that:

1. The labor cost for school mechanics is lower;
2. School maintenance workers have greater pride and interest in the work;
3. School mechanics can be more familiar with the plant;
4. School personnel are available when needed;
5. The hazard of being overcharged by an unscrupulous contractor is avoided;
6. The job can be commenced more promptly.

Those favoring utilizing outside contractors believe that:

1. The school cannot afford to purchase all the needed tools and equipment;
2. The school cannot afford to hire staff members with the necessary high levels of skill;
3. Contract workers are more productive because of the profit motive;
4. Contractors have greater resources to accomplish large volumes of work;
5. The problems of managing skilled personnel are avoided;
6. Schools economize by paying only for the hours that they need and use contractors' personnel.

A variety of local factors determine which plan should be adopted. These factors include size of district, complexity of plant, administrative staffing, labor market, and quality of contractors.

One potential danger faced by school districts which have their own maintenance staff is that district personnel may become involved in large capital projects at the expense of sound maintenance. Although the manpower may have the skills required for such work, diversion of their talents penalizes the periodic maintenance program. As a consequence, the efficiency of operation and the length of useful life of some equipment is often shortened.

Except in the largest of school districts, general practice is to combine both forms of maintenance to gain the maximum advantage. It is frequently found that much routine maintenance is not of a highly skilled nature and can be done most reasonably by district personnel. Examples of these efforts might include grounds maintenance, painting, hardware repairs, motor lubrication, and simple heating, plumbing, and electrical work. Maintenance that requires a highly skilled mechanic or costly equipment for limited periods of time can often be done best by an outside contractor. This could include tasks such as tree-pruning, temperature control system maintenance, clock and bell system service, and elevator maintenance.

CHAPTER VII

Pupil Transportation

Pupil transportation has become an accepted function of school districts in the United States. Transportation does not contribute directly to learning, except as it is used for field trips related to the instructional program. However, it does—particularly in rural and suburban areas—afford conditions for learning that would be inefficient or impossible without it.

The Mandate

Historical development. Transportation of school pupils at public expense began in the mid-nineteenth century as it became apparent that schools could not be located within walking distance of all who were to be educated. During the latter part of the century, more and more states permitted transportation of pupils at school district expense. But it was not until after World War I that this service was to experience significant expansion. The growth in secondary school attendance and the rise in school district consolidations were facilitated by the availability of the gasoline-powered school bus, which had first appeared in 1914, and by the construction of all-weather highways in rural areas.

Since World War II, the increase in transportation has surpassed the boom in student population. The movement of large numbers of families to nonurban areas has resulted in a great increase in pupils who are eligible for bus service. Furthermore, there has been a tendency to reduce the home-to-school distance necessary to qualify the pupil for transportation.

Shortly after World War I, less than 2 per cent of all pupils attending school were being transported at public expense. Today, well over one third of all enrolled pupils are being transported to and from school at district expense.

The result of this growth is a vast and complicated enterprise that is by far the nation's largest transportation operation. Pupil transportation utilizes about 200,000 vehicles to carry close to fifteen million youngsters to and from school each day. Most of these vehicles are buses, ranging in capacity from sixteen to over ninety pupils. Stationwagons and suburbans with capacities between seven and sixteen pupils supplement the larger units. Passenger cars, trucks, motorboats, swamp buggies, and airplanes are also used for school transportation in isolated areas of the nation. Current estimates place the total daily mileage of these vehicles at over six million miles. The annual cost of providing this vast service approximates $550 million.

Legal requirements.   Every state has enacted some legislation authorizing expenditures for pupil transportation. Usually the statutes go considerably beyond approving transportation expenses and stipulate a substantial number of conditions under which service may or must be provided. For example, state laws may require local boards of education to provide transportation to and from the public school if the home-to-school distance exceeds a certain limit.

Frequently state law or state regulation will specify certain qualifications for school bus drivers. Standards for the construction, equipment, inspection, and maintenance of all motor vehicles used for pupil transportation are often mandated by the state.

In most states some degree of discretion is granted to the board of education in the operation of the transportation program.[1] For instance, if the statute designates a distance beyond which transportation must be provided, the local district may have the option of providing service to those residing nearer to the school. If the law stipulates that transportation must be provided on a "reasonable" basis, even wider discretion exists. This may involve defining local service on the basis of such factors as distance, age of pupils, climate, time of day, road conditions, and traffic hazards.

In some states (New York is a notable example) pupil transportation service must be provided to youngsters attending nonpublic schools. When such service is mandated or permitted by state law, the legislation is usually a manifestation of the "child benefit" theory, which postulates that the pupil, rather than the school attended, is

---

[1] Robert L. Drury, (Ed.), *Law and the School Superintendent* (Cincinnati: The W. H. Anderson Co., 1958), Chap. 14.

the beneficiary of activities such as pupil transportation. In a 1947 ruling, the United States Supreme Court upheld the constitutionality of a New Jersey statute that provided parochial school pupils with transportation at public expense.

State support. For the nation as a whole, the financial support of pupil transportation shows a pattern of slightly over one third of the expense met by local district resources and the rest by the state. This is the national average, but there are some states which offer no assistance for any service while others assume all the costs of school transportation.

State assistance is usually in the form of reimbursement to local or intermediate districts for all or a portion of the costs of local transportation programs. In many states the financial support of local transportation is included as a component of the foundation program aid. In others it may be paid under a formula treating pupil transportation as a separate item of local expense. The critical test of any state plan of financial support is not in the method of computation but is in the adequacy of allowances to those school districts which have limited local resources and substantial transportation needs. Failure to provide adequate state support to such communities usually leads either to the diversion of revenues from the instructional program or to substandard operation of the transportation program.

Local policies. Pupil transportation should be organized and operated within a framework of local policies that reflect the school district's standards. In developing local policies, consideration should be given to five criteria:

1. *Safety.* The first consideration of pupil travel must be the safety of the pupils; this should not be compromised in the design or operation of transportation.

2. *Adequacy.* The level of service, the equipment, and staffing must be adequate to provide for the needs of the community and its youth.

3. *Economy.* Since the program is supported by public funds, expenditures for transportation must reflect careful consideration of economy.

4. *Efficiency.* Related to economy is the requirement that service, personnel, and equipment be deployed in such a manner as to achieve maximum performance.

5. *State laws and regulations.* Local policy must support and implement the mandatory elements of state statutes and regulations.

Application of these criteria will inevitably lead to discussions of who shall be transported on what bus schedules and bus routes. Also involved will be the question of public ownership versus use of private contractors or franchised routes.

When these matters have been discussed and decided, the board of education should adopt a set of policies on pupil transportation. The implementation of these policies becomes the responsibility of the superintendent of schools. If the district is large and the transportation operation complex, he may delegate this function to a subordinate administrator.

Local District Programs

Pupil transportation was at first largely in the hands of private operators who contracted with the school district. By the mid-1930's, slightly more than one third of all school buses were district-owned. Today the proportion has been completely reversed, with over 70 per cent of all school buses owned by schools and less than 30 per cent under private contract.

District-owned operation. It is not possible to cite one particular cause for the rise of public ownership and operation of school transportation fleets. Perhaps most important was the recognition by many school administrators and board of education members that the transportation program is intimately related to the educational process.

District ownership normally means that the school district purchases all the vehicles, hires personnel to operate and maintain them, provides suitable maintenance and storage facilities, and purchases parts and supplies essential to the conduct of the program. Because transportation equipment and facilities are costly, they present a capitalization problem for many districts. According to the regulations of the particular state, the impact of these purchases can be spread over a period of years by installment purchasing, lease-purchase arrangements, or the issuance of short-term bonds.

Those who favor district-owned transportation believe it can offer the following advantages:

1. The total operation can be more easily controlled by school administration.

2. Transportation can most easily be integrated with the total educational program.

3. Selection, training, and performance of bus drivers are under direct authority of the school.

4. The system is more adaptable to changes in time schedules, pupil loads, and similar variables.

5. Equipment is readily available for use in transporting pupils on educational field trips and for extracurricular activities.

6. The system provides a permanent program that will be available as long as the school district has the need for transportation.

7. Costs of comparable service are lower under public ownership than under contract operation.

8. Because the school-owned operation is geared toward safety first and economy second, compromises of safety are less apt to occur.

Private contract operation. Although the proportion of pupils being transported by private contract carriers has been decreasing over the past quarter-century, contract operations are still widely used. The utilization of private contractors is strongest in the New England states. Massachusetts, for instance, recently reported that over 95 per cent of its vehicles were owned by private contractors.

Under the private contract method, the school district enters into a contract with one or more contractors for the required pupil transportation, usually after a process of formal or informal bidding. The contract term varies with local needs and state regulation, generally ranging between one and five years. If the contract involves a large amount of capital equipment and considerable staff for operation and maintenance, it is usually advantageous to both the operator and the school district to specify a contract period of longer than one year.

Where private contract operations are employed, they are usually favored for the following reasons:

1. The administrative staff of the school district is relieved of the operational responsibility for transportation. The problems of maintaining vehicles, purchasing supplies, selecting and training bus personnel, establishing routes, and implementing time schedules are assigned to the outside contractor. It can be expected that a large volume of the complaints associated with any pupil transportation operation will be reported directly to and resolved by the contractor.

2. The school district avoids the financial burden of investing in a

large amount of vehicular equipment, tools, and storage facilities. This is a particular problem in a district that undergoes rapid expansion of transportation service, either through growth in enrollments or through liberalization of levels of service. For a school district which transports several thousand pupils, such a capital investment could amount to many hundreds of thousands of dollars.

3. The cost of the transportation service is predictable over the life of the contract. This presumes a contract for an extended period, and one that is secured by a performance bond. Since the bid price is an absolute sum, it is more accurate than any forecast of expenses for several years of district ownership.

Franchised routes. The use of public service transportation is limited to urban areas, where the population density justifies such operations. Where such routes do exist, it is frequently more economical to have the carrier provide transportation for pupils than it would be to undertake a school bus operation, either district-owned or by contract.

Bus Drivers

The bus driver is the most important element in the transportation program. His sound judgment is absolutely essential to safe and efficient operations. Indeed, the driver's influence extends beyond operating the vehicle. He comes into daily contact with each youngster on the bus route. His personality, appearance, and behavior can exert tremendous influences on the pupils in his charge.

Most school districts secure their bus drivers from among the following sources:

1. *Part-time men employees* who have other primary jobs (such as farmers, service station operators, and night-shift workers).
2. *Housewives* who have the strength, skill, and temperament required and who are available part of the day.
3. *Full-time employees* of the school district who are assigned custodial, maintenance, or messenger duties during the other hours of their work day.
4. *Student drivers* who are secondary school pupils, carefully selected and trained and paid a wage for their efforts. (The vast majority of North Carolina's school bus operators are students.)

Qualifications. In selecting personnel to operate school vehicles, the school administrator cannot afford to lose sight of the precious cargo being transported. High standards of competency must be established at the time of employment and maintained during the period of service.

The elemental requirements for these positions should include:

Age. Drivers should have sufficient maturity to operate the vehicle safely and maintain sound passenger discipline. In some states school bus drivers must be twenty-one or over. Several Southern states report excellent results with carefully selected student drivers. Although the use of student drivers is the subject of much debate, there appears to be agreement that extra care is required in selecting, training, and supervising them and that the rate of turnover among such drivers is necessarily high.

Physical condition. Before the driver is hired, he should be given a thorough medical examination. It is desirable to administer a checkup annually. Particular stress should be placed on sound vision and hearing and the absence of cardiovascular defects.

Driving ability. Many states require school vehicle operators to have special licenses. Although previous experience with equipment of similar size and complexity is desired, it is not an overwhelming consideration. It is reasonable to expect that skill can be developed by a local training program.

Character. No school employee should be hired until the administrator is satisfied that the individual is of sound moral character and stable emotional temperament. Since the bus driver is the sole school district employee supervising a large group of youngsters for an extended period of time, this requirement is all the more imperative.

Although the foregoing standards are developed principally for application in district-operated transportation, they are germane to private contract operations. Many school districts stipulate in their contracts with private carriers that the district has the right to approve the selection of bus drivers. If this is not feasible, it would be advantageous to include specific driver qualifications in the contract.

Training and supervision. Training should consist of both pre-service and in-service activities. In most cases, a few days of pre-service training provide the driver with the skill and knowledge necessary for him to perform effectively.

The responsibility for pre-service training can be assigned to the school district's transportation supervisor or head bus driver. Among the topics to be included are:

1. Orientation to the school district and its goals;
2. Explanation of lines of authority and responsibility;
3. Job conditions, salary, fringe benefits;
4. The driver's responsibility for pupil conduct;
5. Orientation to the bus routes;
6. Familiarization with equipment, including daily inspection;
7. Safe driving practices.

In-service activities should be designed to maintain and improve these abilities. Many schools provide a monthly in-service session; others have a more extensive program in the summer. State departments and state universities frequently offer assistance in planning and conducting these activities. Aid is also available from insurance companies, police, utilities companies, and bus manufacturers.

Equipment

Selection of equipment. The modern school bus is a cradle of steel on wheels, expertly designed to transport pupils in comfort and safety. Each year additional improvements are made to improve this equipment. Today all school buses are built to equal or exceed a set of national minimum standards.

Until the late 1930's, school districts were left largely to their own devices in securing adequate school bus design. This resulted in a considerable number of custom-made vehicles which were quite costly and which might or might not have been well engineered. In 1939 Professor Frank W. Cyr of Teachers College, Columbia University, sparked studies, research, and a conference which led to the development of national minimum standards for bus bodies and chassis. This made it possible for school buses to be manufactured on a mass-production scale.

Several times since 1939 these minimum national bus standards have been revised. The most recent such revision occurred in 1959, when the National Conference on School Transportation met and developed a handbook on standards. Most states have adopted and applied these national standards. Some states have inserted certain specific requirements that are even more stringent than the national standards.

Today, most school buses are purchased as assembled units consisting of a standard truck chassis on which another manufacturer's bus body has been mounted. However, more districts are recognizing the merit of "pusher" and transit-type units of integrated construction.

There can be no one unit of a particular size that would represent the wisest purchase for all school districts. The decision for each purchase must reflect such local considerations as:

1. Terrain on the bus route;
2. Climatic conditions in the area;
3. Type of roads;
4. Need for maneuverability;
5. Engine horsepower and torque;
6. Ease of maintenance;
7. Desire for fleet standardization;
8. Availability of service and parts;
9. Life expectancy of vehicles;
10. Cost.

Standards of maintenance. The safe, dependable, comfortable, and economical operation of adequate transportation equipment manned by competent drivers is dependent on a sound maintenance program. Good maintenance will not eliminate all breakdowns, but it will reduce the frequency of such occurrences and extend the useful life of the equipment.

The primary concern in a school bus maintenance program must be to prevent breakdowns rather than to repair failures. Preventive maintenance has three aspects:

1. *First-echelon inspection.* This is the daily attention of the driver to simple inspection and servicing. Proper fuel, oil, and water levels are maintained, electrical equipment and windshield wipers are checked, and tires are visually inspected.

2. *Periodic Service.* This is performed by a mechanic and should follow the manufacturer's service manual in scope and frequency. A checklist and a log of what is performed are essential records in this process. Lubrication, oil changes, and ignition service are the main regular items in periodic service, but other repairs will be performed as required.

3. *Scheduled Overhaul.* This, too, should follow the manufacturer's service manual recommendations, adjusted to local conditions. Depend-

ing on the size and organization of the fleet, this work may be done on the premises or in commercial garages. The need to overhaul a specific component on a particular vehicle is infrequent, usually occurring only two or three times in the vehicle's service life. Typical overhaul tasks are motor rebuilding, transmission repair, and brakes and clutch replacement. Here, too, adequate record keeping is essential.

Some states require periodic inspections of school transportation equipment by designated agencies, at intervals ranging from three months to a year. These inspections should furnish assurance that preventive maintenance has been practiced, rather than seek to discover what defects require correction.

If the school district operates its own transportation equipment, it will have the direct responsibility of seeing that its maintenance program is sound. If the district retains the services of a private contractor, it still has the obligation to see that pupils are transported safely and efficiently. Thus, many such contracts include a requirement that the private contractor adhere to certain maintenance standards.

CHAPTER VIII

School Food Service

Purpose and Goals

Evolution.   It is difficult to pinpoint the start of organized school food service. New York and Philadelphia had limited programs before the Civil War. A new era began in 1894 when the Boston public schools undertook a program of supervised food preparation and service. Within the next twenty years, most of the larger cities made provisions to operate some form of school food services. The primary motivation of early programs was charitable and the major effort was in economically disadvantaged areas.

World War I focused national concern on sound nutrition and school food service spread at a modest rate to smaller cities and suburban and rural areas. Concurrently, the science of nutrition advanced, more became known about sound diet and food preparation, and professional dietitians were trained and became available. The Depression saw a considerable increase in food service, with the program receiving significant federal support.

The greatest impetus in school food service occurred in 1946 when the National School Lunch Act was passed. The Act provides the participating local schools with two forms of aid: a cash reimbursement for each container of milk and each complete meal served; and foodstuffs purchased by the Department of Agriculture (and, in some cases, by states) for consumption in school programs.

It is estimated that considerably over one third of all public elementary and secondary school youngsters now participate in the National School Lunch Program—a vast enterprise constituting the nation's largest food service operation and providing student meals valued at approximately one billion dollars annually.

Philosophy.   The remarkable growth in the scope and quality of school food service has come about as local school authorities, spurred by national and state leadership, realized that the school has a vital role in nutrition. Typically, the schools acknowledge that school lunch programs seek to realize four main goals:

1. *Physical health.* School food service endeavors to maintain and improve the physical health of boys and girls. Sound nutrition contributes to student well-being, which is a prerequisite to maximum learning. Further, children of school age are in their formative years and a diet adequate in kind and amount is essential to proper growth.

2. *Learnings.* The school food service program seeks to help the pupil acquire wholesome eating habits as well as sound diet attitudes. To be most successful, this effort must be accompanied by related classroom instruction. The contribution that the food service program can make is in serving good food that is well prepared and creatively offered for consumption in pleasant surroundings. This tends to reinforce the elements of the instructional program that deal with the importance of sound nutrition.

3. *Social growth.* The lunch hour is generally the principal informal activity of the youngster's school day. Properly organized and conducted, it can be a valuable setting for the social growth of the individual. Pupils are exposed to situations where they are able to practice courtesy to fellow pupils and to gain satisfaction from this behavior.

4. *Attractive pricing.* It is axiomatic in school food service that the youngsters who can gain the most from participating are frequently those who can least afford it. For many pupils who come from homes of limited means, the school lunch is vital to an adequate and balanced diet. Accordingly, the meal price must be maintained at the lowest level consistent with sound economics.

The School Lunch Director

School systems vary in the organization of food services. Typically, very small schools assign the food service operation to the home economics teacher. In medium-sized and larger districts, it is usual to include food service as a business management function. Although the service is usually under the total leadership of the assistant superintendent for business or the business manager, actual management is in the hands of a school lunch director. In more complex operations, the director may have a manager for each of several school lunchrooms or other supervisory assistance.

Qualifications. Like some other positions related to school business management, the position of school lunch director is an emerging one. Efforts are being made to achieve a professional level for this important post, with leadership coming mainly from state education departments and three professional groups: the American Home Economics Association, the American Dietetic Association, and the American School Food Service Association. Membership in the American Home Economics Association is limited to college graduates with a degree in home economics. Similarly, the American Dietetic Association requires of its members a college degree with specialization in this area, coupled with approved experience. However, the American School Food Service Association enrolls all who have an interest in school food service, regardless of their academic training.

Education. A school lunch director should be a college graduate, with undergraduate study in foods, nutrition, institution management, and education. If she is to direct a large operation involving other subordinate professionals, additional formal training is recommended. This should consist of a master's degree in the fields of nutrition, supervision, and management. Whether undergraduate or graduate training is required, the candidate should have had some specific study in school food service.

Experience. Experience requirements should be related to the complexity of the vacant position. Presumably, many inexperienced but trained directors receive their experience in internship programs, in relatively small directorships, or in assistant positions in larger school districts. A reasonable requirement for a full-time director would be one to three years' prior experience involving food service management. (Additional experience might be required in larger operations.)

Responsibilities. The school lunch director has the primary responsibility for planning, organizing, and operating the school food service program. Capable subordinates and understanding superiors make their contributions, but the key to a successful program is the competency of the director. The following are the duties the school lunch director typically performs or shares with or delegates to others:

1. Planning food service facilities, including areas and equipment;
2. Selecting and training food service personnel;
3. Planning and evaluating menus;

4. Supervising the storage, preparation, and servicing of foods;
5. Selecting foodstuffs, supplies, and equipment;
6. Maintaining liaison with federal and state school lunch programs;
7. Establishing and maintaining inventory procedures;
8. Establishing and maintaining procedures for handling of receipts;
9. Establishing sale prices for food items;
10. Preparing cost and participation records on a daily and cumulative basis;
11. Broadening community understanding of the school lunch program;
12. Supervising food preparation and service for extracurricular and outside organizations using school facilities.

Operations

The school district which introduces a food service program may organize and conduct the program with its own employees, or it may contract with an outside agency for the service. Although the food will be distributed on school premises, the district may elect to have the kitchen in the school buildings or at some central location.

Unit kitchens. In most small and medium-sized districts, each school has its own kitchen. Typically, a manager or cook-manager is designated for each such unit. In some cases, the school principal is responsible for management of the program in his building. In others, the operation of all school cafeterias is the responsibility of a districtwide director who operates in close cooperation with each principal in establishing the food service program for each building.

Central kitchens. This plan concentrates food purchasing, menu planning, and meal preparation in one or more central locations. Vehicles with specially designed vacuum containers and heated compartments are used to distribute the food to the individual schools.

Central kitchens have gained initial acceptance in the largest cities, where they have generally been successful. But more and more smaller cities, with no more than 100 or 150 cafeteria employees, are investigating this method of food preparation.

Among the possible advantages of a central kitchen operation are:

1. Lower labor costs because of more efficient methods of food preparation;
2. Better purchasing and inventory control;
3. Uniformly high quality standards;
4. Reduced total expenditures for food preparation equipment because of the elimination of unit kitchens in individual schools;
5. Considerably less space required in the school buildings.

Commercial concession. The idea of having an outside firm manage on-premises food service is not new; many early school lunch programs followed this practice. But the plan lost favor and many cities and most suburban and rural school food programs became school-operated activities. The major reasons that school administrators look with disfavor on food services by a commercial concessionaire are:

1. The school cannot control the quality of food, its method of preparation and service, or the personnel involved in the program.
2. The concessionaire must operate at a profit to remain in business. This can lead to inadequate portions, poor selection of menu items, and prices that discourage desired participation.
3. Commercial operations receive no National School Lunch Act assistance; presumably this results in higher meal prices.

Vending machines. A new concept of operation, showing promise of future growth, is the use of vending machines in school food service programs. Many schools use vending machines to dispense beverages and snacks; some are experimenting with machines to serve full meals. The food for machine vending can be purchased in ready-to-consume portions or it can be prepared and packaged in the school district's central kitchen. Vending machines may enable schools to capitalize on the rapid advances that are occurring in the processing, packaging, and preservation of food.

Among the potential advantages claimed for vending machines are:

1. There is no need to have kitchens in each school, permitting realization of significant savings in space and facilities.
2. Fewer personnel are required for food preparation and service in the school, resulting in lower labor costs per meal.
3. Actual service is more rapid, since children do not pass through the usual cafeteria line.

Operating Personnel

Operating personnel include the cooks, bakers, salad makers, food service helpers, dishwashers, cashiers, stock clerks, and others who comprise the food preparation and service effort. These staff members will have wide ranges in skill, in degree of responsibility, and in ability to grow with the operation.

Selection and qualifications. A few districts secure as personnel graduates of secondary school vocational or home economics courses. But the main reservoir of food service personnel is the large pool of married women in the community.

Although some positions may require specific competencies, most food service applicants can be selected on the basis of four major criteria:

Health. Good health, both physical and mental, should be a cardinal requirement for initial employment and continued service. At entrance and annually thereafter, a complete physical examination should be required.

Age. The food service task is an active assignment and will require women of reasonable strength and vitality. Chronological age of itself is a poor criterion to determine these attributes. Generally, age eligibility for food service work can follow the local requirement for general public employment, and concern should center on ability to perform.

Appearance. Neat personal appearance is a necessity because food service personnel are the human element in the pupils' dining environment. A healthy complexion, good grooming, and neat attire are essentials if the employee is to contribute to pleasant surroundings.

Intelligence and personality. A food service staff member should have sufficient intelligence to learn her duties and discharge them dependably and with limited supervision. A pleasant, stable personality is needed, not only for healthy relationships with fellow workers, but also for contacts with students.

Training. The great majority of food service staff members come to the job without previous experience in quantity food preparation and service. This mandates an active program of training to provide new workers with basic skills, to increase total staff proficiency, and to upgrade specific individuals to more responsible positions.

The nature of the training varies from a formal, organized preservice or in-service program to simple on-the-job learnings. Preservice training is a goal desired by many directors but achieved by few, since selection rarely precedes actual need.

Every new employee should receive some on-the-job training. At first this consists mainly of orientation to fellow staff members, to the physical layout of the kitchen, and to the plan of operation. As the worker becomes more relaxed in the new surroundings, she should be introduced to more complex assignments. When an employee reveals particular talent, plans should be made to provide added skill by formal and informal instruction.

Formal in-service training programs may be conducted on a districtwide basis in larger districts. Smaller districts often seek assistance from state education departments, universities, vocational programs, adult education programs, other school districts, and professional organizations.

Performance standards. Since labor rates are rising each year, while food costs remain fairly stable, the development of performance standards is absolutely essential. This is the responsibility of the director and involves providing adequate tools, equipment, and environment and coordinating individual efforts.

It is impossible to develop a blanket rule on the number of staff members required for a given number of meals. The caliber of the workers, the adequacy of kitchen facilities, the degree of centralization, and the number and kinds of à la carte items contribute to variances in labor needs. George and Heckler[1] indicate that a secondary school offering a plate lunch and à la carte items can expect to prepare and serve between six and ten meals per hour of staff labor, with the highest production in schools serving a large number of meals.

Record Keeping

Need. As the school food service enterprise has increased in volume and complexity, it has been recognized that a system of

---

[1] N. L. George and Ruth D. Heckler, *School Food Centers* (New York: The Ronald Press Company, 1960).

accounting, reporting, and record keeping is necessary for sound management. Records should be as simple as possible while providing necessary details. In addition, they should be maintained on the basis of clearly defined rules and procedures. Adequate records can perform these functions:

1. Serve as a control on the handling of supply inventory, to prevent loss due to waste, theft, or improper ordering;
2. Become the basis for reporting food service activities to local and state authorities;
3. Provide documentation of worthy stewardship;
4. Furnish needed intelligence for reaching managerial decisions;
5. Provide information for ordering supplies.

Types of records. Three main categories of records will be required: financial, participation, and performance. Ordinarily the chief records for these purposes will be kept under the supervision of the Director. Some of these records will be integrated with records of functions conducted elsewhere in the business affairs division of the school district. For example, employee time sheets may be combined with payroll records, while statements of school lunch expenditures may become a part of a report of all school financial activities.

Financial records involve income and expense. If the food service program is operated by the board of education, all cafeteria income is usually considered public funds. Accordingly, the same safeguards and controls are required in handling and accounting for school lunch monies as are mandated for the district's general fund. School food service receipts and disbursements can be included in the general fund, but are more usually segregated in a special fund.

Participation records reflect the volume and kind of meals and à la carte food items served to the patrons of the program. Performance records indicate food and supply purchases, consumption rates, and labor volume and distribution. Combined with financial records, these provide the necessary data for analysis and control of funds, materials, and personnel.

The principal records include:

1. *Daily cash receipts records.* These indicate the income from food sales each day and can be reconciled with cash register tapes.
2. *Cash receipts and expenditure journal.* This is maintained in

chronological order and cumulatively. Summaries are prepared monthly for reports.

3. *Voucher and check register.* This indicates the essential data on each payment for supplies and outside services.

4. *Profit and loss statement.* This is prepared monthly throughout the school year. It summarizes cash receipts, cash reimbursements, and values of surplus commodities from state and federal support programs, patronage, payroll costs, and costs of purchases of food and outside services.

5. *Inventory record.* This reports the amount and value of food and supplies on hand at the start of each month, less consumption and plus purchases occurring during month, to indicate end-of-month position.

6. *Cost-per-meal analysis.* This provides a detailed breakdown of the cost of food, labor, and supplies reduced to a unit basis for a particular meal. Similar analysis on a per-portion basis can be made of individual menu items.

7. *Staff performance record.* This indicates the employees, assignments, hours of duty, and attendance and absence. This information is recorded daily and submitted to the business office periodically for payroll preparation.

8. *Daily patronage record.* This indicates the number and kinds of foods served to adult and student patrons. It becomes the basis for participation in federal and state support programs.

Bibliography

Association of School Business Officials of the United States and Canada, *Annual Volume of Proceedings, 1928–62*. Evanston, Ill.: The Association, 1928–62.

——, *Fire Insurance Principles and Practices*. Evanston, Ill.: The Association, 1958.

——, *The School Business Administrator*. Evanston, Ill.: The Association, 1960.

——, *Purchasing and Supply Management Manual for School Business Officials*, Bulletin No. 22. Evanston, Ill.: The Association, 1962.

Drury, Robert L. (Ed.), *Law and the School Superintendent*. Cincinnati: The W. H. Anderson Co., 1958.

Finchum, R. N., *School Plant Management—Administering the Custodial Program*, U.S. Office of Education Bulletin 1961, No. 4. Washington, D.C.: USGPO, 1960.

Finchum, R. N. and N. E. Viles, *School Insurance—Managing the Local Program*, U.S. Office of Education Bulletin 1959, No. 23. Washington, D.C.: USGPO, 1959.

George, N. L. and Ruth D. Heckler, *School Food Centers*. New York: The Ronald Press Company, 1960.

Good, H. G., *A History of American Education*. New York: The Macmillan Company, 1956.

Griffiths, Daniel E., *Administrative Theory*. New York: Appleton-Century-Crofts, Inc., 1959.

Griffiths, Daniel E., David L. Clark, D. Richard Wynn, and Laurence Iannaccone, *Organizing Schools for Effective Education*. Danville, Ill.: The Interstate Printers & Publishers, Inc., 1962.

Hamilton, Robert R. and Paul R. Mort, *The Law and Public Education*. Brooklyn, N.Y.: The Foundation Press, Inc., 1959.

Hamilton, Robert R. and E. Edmund Reutter, Jr., *Legal Aspects of School Board Operation*. New York: Teachers College, Bureau of Publications, Columbia University, 1958.

Johns, Roe L. and Edgar L. Morphet, *Financing the Public Schools*. Englewood Cliffs, N.J.: Prentice-Hall, Inc., 1960.

Knezevich, Stephen J. and John Guy Fowlkes, *Business Management of Local School Systems*. New York: Harper & Row, Publishers, 1960.

Linn, Henry H. (Ed.), *School Business Administration*. New York, The Ronald Press Company, 1956.

Linn, Henry H. and Schuyler E. Joyner, *Insurance Practices in School Administration*. New York: The Ronald Press Company, 1952.

Morphet, Edgar L., Roe L. Johns, and Theodore L. Reller, *Educational Administration*. Englewood Cliffs, N.J.: Prentice-Hall, Inc., 1959.

Mort, Paul R., Walter C. Reusser, and John W. Polley, *Public School Finance*. New York: McGraw-Hill, Inc., 1960.

Ovsiew, Leon and William B. Castetter, *Budgeting for Better Schools*. Englewood Cliffs, N.J.: Prentice-Hall, Inc., 1960.

Reason, Paul L. and George G. Tankard, Jr., *Property Accounting for Local and State School Systems*. U.S. Office of Education Bulletin 1959, No. 22. Washington, D.C.: USGPO, 1959.

Reason, Paul L. and Alpheus L. White, *Financial Accounting for Local and State School Systems, Standard Receipts and Expenditure Accounts*. U.S. Office of Education Bulletin 1957, No. 4. Washington, D.C.: USGPO, 1957.

Ritterskamp, James J., Jr., Forrest L. Abbott, and Bert C. Ahrens (Eds.), *Purchasing for Educational Institutions*. New York: Teachers College, Bureau of Publications, Columbia University, 1961.

Roe, William H., *School Business Management*. New York: McGraw-Hill Book Company, Inc., 1961.

Samuelson, Everett V., George G. Tankard, Jr., and Hoyt W. Pope, *Financial Accounting for School Activities*. U.S. Office of Education Bulletin 1959, No. 21. Washington, D.C.: USGPO, 1959.

Strevell, Wallace H. and Arvid J. Burke, *Administration of the School Building Program*. New York: McGraw-Hill Book Company, Inc., 1959.

Tidwell, Sam B., *Public School Fund Accounting*. New York: Harper & Row, Publishers, 1960.

Walton, John, *Administration and Policy-Making in Education*. Baltimore: The Johns Hopkins Press, 1959.

Yeager, William A., *Administration of the Noninstructional Personnel and Services*. New York: Harper & Row, Publishers, 1959.

Index